INVEST WITH THE HOUSE

HACKING THE TOP HEDGE FUNDS

MEB FABER

INVEST WITH THE HOUSE

Hacking the Top Hedge Funds

ISBN 978-0-9886799-8-6

COVER DESIGN BY ERIN TYLER & OANA ROXANA

INTERIOR DESIGN BY IAN CLAUDIUS

to JAQ *and* D

CONTENTS

APPENDICES

ABOUT THE AUTHOR

Mr. Faber is a co-founder and the Chief Investment Officer of Cambria Investment Management, LP. Faber is the manager of Cambria's ETFs, separate accounts, and private investment funds for accredited investors. Mr. Faber is also the author of the Meb Faber Research blog, *Shareholder Yield*, *Global Value*, *Global Asset Allocation* and the co-author of *The Ivy Portfolio: How to Invest Like the Top Endowments and Avoid Bear Markets*. He is a frequent speaker and writer on investment strategies and has been featured in *Barron's*, *The New York Times*, and *The New Yorker*. Mr. Faber graduated from the University of Virginia with degrees in Engineering Science and Biology. He is a Chartered Alternative Investment Analyst (CAIA), and Chartered Market Technician (CMT).

Contact Information

Twitter: @MebFaber
Email: Mebane@gmail.com
Phone: 310-683-5500
Blog: mebfaber.com
Research: theideafarm.com
Company: cambriafunds.com

ACKNOWLEDGEMENTS

Many years ago, an investor had to track and backtest US Securities and Exchange Commission (SEC) filings by hand, a truly arduous task. I helped cofound a company with Mazin Jadallah in 2008 called AlphaClone to help automate the process. Thanks to Maz and the team at AlphaClone for providing the backtest and holdings data that I use throughout the book. While it has been years since I have been involved with the company, in full disclosure, I still retain a small passive equity stake.

I would like to thank Irwin Speizer for his thoughtful assistance with editing and writing this book. Also thanks to the many research boutiques and investment companies for providing their own insights and feedback included in the text.

Many friends and family helped in editing my terrible grammar and spelling. Also thanks to Professor Griffin for the original inspiration for this book over 15 years ago.

CHAPTER 1

THE CASINO CAN BE BEAT

"I believe in the discipline of mastering the best that other people have ever figured out. I don't believe in just sitting there and trying to dream it up all yourself. Nobody's that smart."

— CHARLIE MUNGER

Stock picking is hard—really, really, hard. The odds are stacked against you. My friends at Longboard Asset Management completed a study called "The Capitalism Distribution" that examined stock returns from the top 3,000 stocks from 1983–2007.[1] They found that:

- 64 percent of stocks underperformed the broad stock market index,
- 39 percent of stocks were unprofitable investments,
- 19 percent of stocks lost at least 75 percent of their value, and
- 25 percent of stocks were responsible for all the market's gains.

Simply picking a stock out of a hat means you have a 64 percent chance of underperforming a basic index fund and a 39 percent chance of losing money!

Not only is it hard to pick stocks, but you are also up against the most talented investors in the world—people like Ray Dalio, founder of Bridgewater Associates, the world's largest hedge fund. Dalio is fond of comparing stock market investing to a poker game, and his description brings to mind the old saying that "if you sit down at the poker table and you don't know who the sucker is, then you're the sucker." Dalio has spent oodles of time and money to make sure he's not the sucker. Here's how Dalio once described his investment methods using the poker analogy:

"The bets are zero sum. In order for you to beat me in the game, it's like poker; it's a zero-sum game. We have 1,500 people that work at Bridgewater, we spend hundreds of millions of dollars on research, and so on. We've been doing this for 37 years, and we don't know that we're going to win. We have to have diversified bets. So it's very important for most people to know when not to make a bet. Because if you're going to come to the poker table, you're going to have to beat me, and you're going to have to beat those who take money. So the nature of investing is that a very small percentage of the people take money, essentially, in that poker game away from other people who don't know when prices go up, whether that means it's a good investment or if it's a more expensive investment."

With his superior stable of research and investment talent, Dalio figures he can beat most of the other players at the table. And he does. His Bridgewater fund posts investment returns that make others jealous. He does it year after year. Here's what's really interesting: he is not the only one. A special few have done it as well, beating the market year after year. They don't all do it the same way or with the same investments; some have done it better than others, and some eventually falter. But the fact is, it happens, and it does so with some consistency.

We make two assumptions that are vital to the arguments in this book:

1. There are active managers that can beat the market (i.e., the market is not completely efficient).

2. Superior active managers can be identified.

These two concepts are difficult for many investors to swallow. There is a general feeling that the market can't be beat, and it is tough to get past that belief. A big challenge is separating luck from skill. But would anyone deny that some people are better than others at stock picking? Just like any other profession, the investment field has top experts who are paid handsomely for what they do.

Warren Buffett of Berkshire Hathaway certainly comes to mind. Buffett is one of the most famous stock pickers of all time, and with an estimated net worth of more than $70 billion, he is also one of the richest people in the world. The 2014 Berkshire Hathaway annual report indicates that the per-share market value of the company has increased at a compounded annual rate of 21.6 percent since 1965. Compared to an average of 9.9 percent for the S&P 500, including dividends, the outperformance is striking.

In June 2014, Andy Chua, a businessman from Singapore, paid over $2 million in a charity auction to have lunch with Buffett, but it's possible to learn some of Buffett's wisdom for a lot less. In fact, it's possible to learn what stocks he is buying and selling for free.

One of the basic principles of the US stock market is transparency, and it is a characteristic that has helped make our stock market so attractive to investors around the world. Of course, it isn't always transparent, and there are noticeable lapses and scandals and shenanigans. But in one particular area, transparency works very well, and it is this area that forms the data source for this book. Under SEC rules, any professional fund manager with more than $100 million in US-listed assets must report stock holdings. That means great stock pickers, such as Warren Buffett, must disclose their stock picks. You may already be aware of this, but many are not.

Thanks to the Internet, you can now look up any of these fund holdings online from the SEC website. It is one of the most valuable sources of market information around. It is simple and easy to access, and it gives you a window into the trading activity of the greatest managers. Sadly, not many investors take advantage of it. Instead, most investors get their investment information from their brokers or TV talking heads, or they pick up a stock tip from a friend or neighbor. As a recent TIAA-CREF study illustrates, people spend more time picking a restaurant or researching which TV to buy than they do planning their retirement investments.

But consider what you get when you examine these SEC filings. You have access to the stock picks made by fund managers who often spend millions of dollars and every waking moment thinking and obsessing about the financial markets. If you think this statement is an exaggeration, note that there are hedge fund managers who lease satellites to track department store traffic and resulting sales estimates.

These stock picks are the result of painstaking work done by people significantly more capitalized than you, who have way more resources than you do, and who, if you select the right ones, are way better than you at picking stocks. The best ones know everything there is to know about a company before they invest. Lee Ainslie, portfolio manager at Maverick Capital (which I examine later in the book), has this to say about how obsessive Julian Robertson of Tiger Management was when examining companies:

"Julian was maniacal on the importance of management: 'Have you done your work on management?' Yes, sir. 'Where did the CFO go to college?' Umm, umm. 'I thought you did your work?' He wanted you to know everything there was to know about the people running the companies you invested in." (The Idea Farm)

This is your competition! Do *you* know where the CFO went to college? Do you even know *who* the CFO is? Do you even know *what* a CFO is? (In case you don't, it's a chief financial officer.)

To go back to the poker analogy, examining SEC filings is like getting a peek at the cards held by these investment managers. It's a great way to learn from some of the brightest investment minds in the world—would you rather play with them, or against them?

This book will begin by examining a case study of how an investor could have followed Buffett's stock picks to great success. We will examine the performance of his stock picks in the past to determine how well they performed, a process called back-testing. This can tell you how you might have fared if you had piggybacked on Buffett's stock picks in the past. While backtesting doesn't tell you how a manager will perform in the future, it does give you a record of performance from which you can draw your own conclusions. Logic suggests that a manager who outperforms consistently must be pretty good at what he does. Will he do it again next year? No one ever knows for sure. But again, logic suggests the odds are in your favor if you select and follow a manager who has a demonstrated record of success and then prudently add some of his stock picks to your own portfolio. Buffett is an obvious choice to start with.

Buffett is the first of twenty of the best investors in the world whose backgrounds and track records we will examine. I provide a brief overview of the process of following these star managers, along with some case studies that demonstrate the managers' stock picks in detail and how the portfolios would have performed since the year 2000. You can then build a stable of these managers and use them as your own personal "idea farm" for stock ideas to research and possibly implement in your own portfolio. The process I outline is an effective way to track and potentially copy the stock picks of some of the best stock pickers in the world.

So let's get started.

CHAPTER 2

BERKSHIRE HATHAWAY, WARREN BUFFETT, AND CHARLIE MUNGER

"Techniques shrouded in mystery clearly have value to the purveyor of investment advice. After all, which witch doctor has ever achieved fame and fortune by simply advising, 'Take two aspirins'?"

— WARREN BUFFETT

Warren Buffett is one of the most famous investors of all time, and his Omaha-based Berkshire Hathaway is one of the most successful investment companies ever. Buffett's financial pronouncements are so revered that they have earned him the nickname "The Sage of Omaha." Buffett practices a style of stock selection called value investing, and he has always given credit for his success to the techniques and principles he learned from his mentor, Benjamin Graham, author of the legendary tomes *Security Analysis* (first published in 1939) and *The Intelligent Investor* (first published in 1949). Graham ran his own investment partnership for years, grounded on the concept of buying stocks that were cheap compared to their intrinsic values. He preached about buying securities that had a "margin of safety."

But while Buffett has spent his life making money through value investing, Graham ended up reconsidering some of the basic tenets of the practice. Graham decided that the investment world had changed so much over time that markets had become much more efficient, making it too difficult to make money by looking for undervalued stock gems. He began to adopt the efficient market hypothesis, which holds that the market is so efficient that stock prices always incorporate and reflect all relevant information, which makes it all but impossible to beat the market through stock selection. Graham discusses his conversion to market efficiency in an article in the *Financial Analysts Journal* (1976):

"I am no longer an advocate of elaborate techniques of security analysis in order to find superior value opportunities. This was a rewarding activity, say, 40 years ago, when our textbook *Graham and Dodd* was first published; but the situation has changed a great deal since then. In the old days any well-trained security analyst could do a good professional job of selecting undervalued issues through detailed studies; but in the light of the enormous amount of research now being carried on, I doubt whether in most cases such extensive efforts will generate sufficiently superior selections to justify their cost. To that very limited extent I'm on the side of the 'efficient market' school of thought now generally accepted by the professors."

And Graham came to this conclusion prior to the advent of the Internet, Bloomberg, and other modern research tools! The efficient market hypothesis (EMH) that was making the rounds through academia and the investing public at the time suggests it is nearly impossible to beat the market through stock selection.

Buffett on Market Efficiency

EMH is where Buffett and his mentor part ways. Buffett has famously dismissed the EMH, stating, "I'd be a bum on the street with a tin cup if the markets were always efficient." For Buffet's style of value investing to be successful, the efficient market theory must not be valid. If it were, there would be no value stocks to be found. Buffett himself has said, "The disservice done to students and gullible investment professionals who have swallowed EMH has been an extraordinary service to us" (Hagstrom, *The Warren Buffett Way: Investment Strategies of the World's Greatest Investor*).

It is my view that Buffett is correct on this point, and for proof, one need look no further than his investment record or the records of any of a number of successful managers who employ a similar value investing style that seeks to capitalize on market inefficiency. Today, an investor who wants exposure to Buffett's investing acumen can invest in any of a number of mutual funds that share the Buffett investment style. When Buffett closed his early investment partnership in 1969, he advised his investors to place their money in the Sequoia Fund, managed by Ruane, Cuniff & Goldfarb, Inc. (which reopened in 2008 for the first time since 1985 but is now closed again). The fund returned over 14 percent a year from 1970 to 2013, besting the S&P 500 by over 3 percentage points per year. The Tweedy Browne family of funds is another good example—in fact, several employees of the old Graham-Newman partnership founded the firm.

While Warren Buffett has gone on to deploy hedge fund techniques such as currency and commodity trading, merger arbitrage, convertible arbitrage, catastrophe bonds, PIPEs, and private equity, he is known mostly for his stock picks. There have been numerous books that have tried to divine exactly how Buffett goes about selecting his investments. The American Association of Individual Investors (AAII) and Validea Capital Management have developed screens that are designed to find companies that Warren Buffett would buy based on criteria he has promoted through decades of public speaking, annual reports, and prior transactions. AQR Capital even published a whitepaper entitled

"Buffett's Alpha" that attempts to distill his process down to an algorithm. Some investors simply buy Berkshire Hathaway stock, gaining access to his portfolio management skills, exposure to the operations of an insurance conglomerate, and entry into the Berkshire Hathaway annual shareholder meeting (which I highly recommend attending!).

But why not just buy what Warren buys? We set out in this chapter to examine whether following Berkshire Hathaway's investments through government filings could offer the investor the opportunity to piggyback on Buffett's stock picks, and consequently, achieve outsized returns. We will get there shortly. But first, a little background.

What Is Form 13F?

In 1975 Congress passed Section 13(f) pursuant to the Securities Exchange Act of 1934. The measure required the manager of every institutional fund with assets under management over $100 million to report its holdings to the Securities and Exchange Commission once a quarter. Congress enacted this legislation to improve the disclosure and transparency of these big firms with the hopes of increasing confidence in the financial markets.

In the early days, accessing these records—called Form 13F or Form 13F-HR—was difficult and tedious. But with the advent of the Internet, everything changed. These days, the forms are uploaded to the SEC website, and an investor can view the holdings 45 days after the quarter's end. By reviewing the 13Fs, you can see and dissect the holdings of every manager from George Soros to Seth Klarman and Carl Icahn to Warren Buffett—all for free.

The SEC maintains these filings on its EDGAR database and posts the electronic versions of 13F filings within a day of receiving the filings.[2] Other websites, including EDGAR Online, Bloomberg, and FactSet/LionShares, aggregate the information into more useable and searchable formats, often for a fee. The electronic data go back to late 1999, although the archives in Washington, DC contain paper records that go back further. (We mention more websites in the back of this book under Resources.) Figure 1 shows part of a page that would come up in a general search for Berkshire Hathaway on the SEC's EDGAR site.

FIGURE 1 – SEC EDGAR WEBSITE

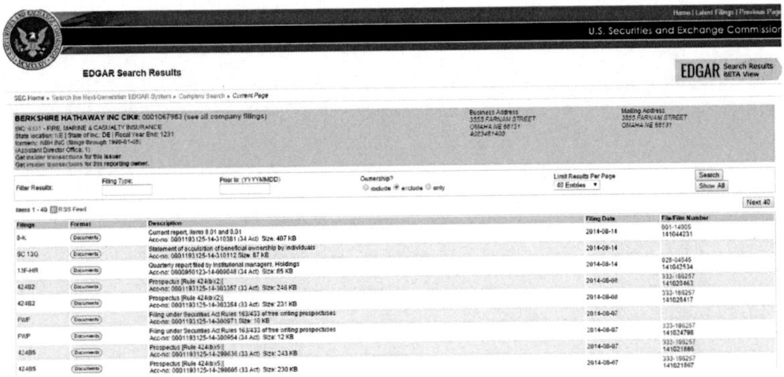

Source: SEC.

To reach the Berkshire filings page, all an investor has to do is to visit the SEC website and search under Company Name for "Berkshire Hathaway." A laundry list of filings will pop up. You can search through them for the 13Fs. Or you can narrow the search by entering "13F" in the Form Type box, which puts all the of the quarterly 13F filings at your fingertips.

Since the 13Fs are published within 45 days after a quarter's end, the quarter that ended June 30, 2015, would be available around August 15, 2015. Examining this 13F from Berkshire reveals a list of longtime Buffett holdings, including American Express, Wells Fargo, and Coca-Cola. It also includes newer names, such as IBM. Remember that the names in the portfolio represent Buffett's collaboration with Charlie Munger as well as his two new portfolio managers, Ted Weschler and Todd Combs.

Note, however, that the SEC filing format is difficult to read and comprehend. A number of websites that publish the current holdings in a more readable format have launched. We mention a list of such sites in Appendix A. Below is my version of simplifying the data into a much more readable chart.

FIGURE 2 – 13F CURRENT HOLDINGS AS OF SEPTEMBER 30, 2015; PRICE AS OF NOVEMBER 20, 2015

Company	Symbol	Price	% of Portfolio
Wells Fargo & Co	WFC	$55.82	19%
Kraft Heinz Co	KHC	$73.65	18%
Coca-Cola Co	KO	$42.43	13%
International Business Machines Corp	IBM	$138.50	9%
American Express Co	AXP	$72.42	9%
Phillips 66	PSX	$91.67	4%
Procter & Gamble Co	PG	$75.82	3%
Wal Mart Stores Inc	WMT	$60.07	3%
U.S. Bancorp	USB	$44.04	3%
DaVita HealthCare Partners Inc	DVA	$73.53	2%

Source: AlphaClone.

This information is indeed interesting, but can it be of any value? The data is forty-five-days "stale" when you see it, and the manager may very well not even own a particular stock by the time the 13F is posted. In addition, he may have added a stock at the start of the ninety-day reporting cycle, so a "new" stock could have been purchased as long as 135 days ago. To further muddy the waters, some managers game the system by omitting certain recently acquired holdings and then filing amended 13F forms later.

But even with all those delays, there is plenty of rich data here that you can use. By sticking with managers who have long holding periods, the delay in reporting times should not be a major factor in your own performance if you try to piggyback. In Buffett's case, he has stated that his favorite holding period is "forever," so turnover should not be a big issue. The major value added in the investment process from the managers this book will examine is in stock picking, not in market timing. The portfolios I will track are long only. Most hedge funds also short and/or use derivatives to hedge or leverage their ideas. But these positions do not show up on the 13F filing, so they will not concern us here.

The methodology I am going to use is as follows:

1. Download all of the 13F quarterly filings back to January 2000.

2. Create historical stock portfolios, including all stocks that are no longer traded due to delistings, buyouts, mergers, bankruptcies, etc. I also include all dividends (cash, stock, special, etc.).

3. I equal-weight the top ten holdings with a 10 percent weight for each stock. In reality, if there are more than ten holdings, I will simply use the ten largest holdings, as the majority of a manager's performance should be driven by his largest holdings. Investors could also weight the holdings similarly to how the manager weighs his portfolio, but I am using a simple example for the book. In reality, it doesn't matter that much.

4. Rebalance, add/delete holdings quarterly, and calculate performance as of the twentieth day of the month to allow for all filings to arrive.

It is not realistic for an individual investor to go and do this work on his or her own. Even finding a historical stock database would be problematic. The good news is that I have done the work for you, and you can follow along in the pages that follow.

Using the methodology presented above, the simulated results for the period from 2000 to 2014 are found in Figure 3. For backtesting, I assume an investor would have bought the top ten stocks in the clone portfolio in 2000, and if any were sold by Buffett, they would have been replaced with his new buys every quarter.

The Clone column represents the Berkshire strategy portfolio with ten holdings equal-weighted and rebalanced quarterly. I use data provided by AlphaClone to produce my models, so in all subsequent strategy charts, the Clone column represents the fund under discussion. I chose to compare Berkshire returns to the broad US market (S&P 500).

The first observation is how mediocre the returns have been for US stocks the past fifteen years (less than 5 percent per year with 50 percent drawdowns) and how much better the Berkshire portfolio performed, with a 10.5 percent return and 43 percent drawdowns. Drawdowns measure the peak to trough loss a portfolio experiences, and I measure that here at the monthly timeframe. The Sharpe ratio is a measure of risk-adjusted return. (Technically, the formula is [Return – T-Bill return]/ Volatility.)

Typically, asset classes like US stocks or bonds tend to cluster around the 0.2 to 0.3 range. The 0.61 for the clone portfolio is much higher than the 0.16 for the broad US stock market.

Buffett's equity selections outperformed the indices quite substantially. Volatility was reasonable, which is surprising given that the portfolio only contained ten holdings. If you ran a mutual fund with these numbers, you would be one of the best-performing managers in the United States!

A study by Gerald Martin and John Puthenpurackal entitled "Imitation is the Sincerest Form of Flattery: Warren Buffett and Berkshire Hathaway" found that a similar method to our simple clone above would have resulted in returns over ten percentage points a year higher than the S&P 500 from 1976 to 2006.[3] A more recent paper entitled "Buffett's Alpha" attempts to build a quant screen similar to Buffett's methods (in addition to 13F tracking portfolios) and finds that both do quite well.[4]

One question many readers often ask is, "How does the cloning strategy perform versus just buying Berkshire stock?" Below is the same 13F top ten clone versus owning Berkshire A shares.

2000-2014	Clone	S&P 500
Return	10.53%	4.31%
Volatility	14.19%	15.24%
Sharpe (1.83%)	0.61	0.16
Drawdown	-42.98%	-50.95%

Year	Clone	S&P 500	Difference
2000	22.8%	-8.2%	31.0%
2001	5.4%	-11.9%	17.3%
2002	-0.9%	-22.1%	21.2%
2003	26.8%	28.7%	-1.9%
2004	10.9%	10.9%	-0.0%
2005	7.3%	4.9%	2.4%
2006	21.7%	15.8%	5.9%
2007	-2.1%	5.5%	-7.6%
2008	-19.0%	-37.0%	18.0%
2009	21.0%	26.5%	-5.5%
2010	13.9%	15.1%	-1.2%
2011	11.5%	2.1%	9.4%
2012	12.4%	16.0%	-3.6%
2013	25.8%	32.4%	-6.6%
2014	10.8%	13.7%	-2.9%

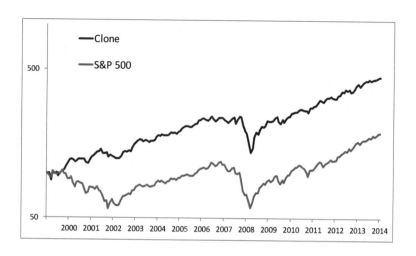

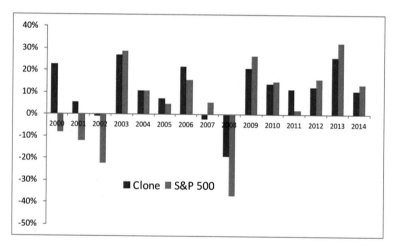

Source: AlphaClone.

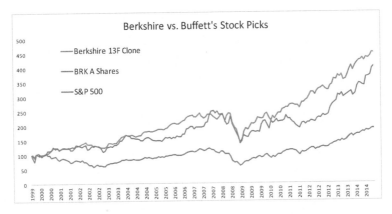

Source: AlphaClone.

The good news is, either strategy worked great and beat the S&P 500 by about 4-5 percentage points per year. And note, that outperformance has occurred while Buffett and Berkshire have underperformed the S&P 500 since the bottom in 2009. Buffett often gains much of his outperformance during bear markets. The best news? You can allocate to Buffett and not pay any hedge or mutual fund fees!

Now that we have a decent base case upon which to build, in the next chapter, we will examine some of the pros and cons of following 13Fs.

CHAPTER 3

THE GOOD AND BAD ABOUT A 13F STRATEGY

"My mantra is diversity. I clone my mentors. I copy everything they do, and then I innovate on top of it."

— HENRY MARKRAM

To summarize some of the differences in managing a portfolio based on 13F filings versus allocating an investment to an active hedge fund manager, the following list is helpful.

PROS of using 13Fs

1. **Access** – Many of the best hedge funds are not open to new investment capital, and if they are, many have high minimum requirements (in excess of $10 million in many cases). As Mark Yusko of Morgan Creek Capital says in *Foundations and Endowment Investing*, "We don't want to give money to people that want our money. We want to give it to people that don't want

it." A 13F tracking strategy allows investors to follow otherwise inaccessible managers.

2. **Transparency** – The investor controls and is aware of the exact holdings at all times. If an investor was following hedge fund Galleon Group during its insider trading scandal, the investor could simply sell his or her stocks rather than wait to redeem their allocation.

3. **Liquidity** – The investor can trade out of positions at any time versus the monthly, quarterly, or multi-year lockup periods at hedge funds. Hedge funds have other special provisions like gates, which can be put up to prevent investors from withdrawing money immediately. Many investors were gated during the financial crisis when they wanted to withdraw their investments.

4. **Lower fees** – Most funds charge high fees (the standard is 2 percent management and 20 percent performance fees). Funds of funds layer on an additional 1 percent and 10 percent. The fees associated with managing a 13F portfolio are simply the investor's routine brokerage expenses.

5. **Risk targeting** – Investors can control the hedging and leverage to suit their risk tolerances. A number of hedge funds have "blown up" as a result of excessive risk from leverage or derivatives.

6. **Fraud avoidance** – Investors own and independently custody their assets, thus completely avoiding any custody risks like those in the Bernie Madoff scheme, in which investors lost billions.

7. **Tax management** – Hedge funds typically run their strategies

without regard to tax implications, while individual investors can manage their positions in accordance with their respective tax statuses.

The impacts of fees and tax management are often minimized when talking about hedge funds since the nominal returns are the sexy part of the story. I cover the importance of taxes and fees in my recent book *Global Asset Allocation*. There is a great paper on this topic, "Rules of Prudence for Individual Investors," by Mark Kritzman of Windham Capital.[5] The underreported story is that taxes have a significant impact on returns for the taxable investor. A hedge fund needs to return about 19 percent to deliver the same after-tax return as a stock index fund that returns 10 percent! (This is due to high turnover resulting in capital gains as well as large performance fees in the hedge fund.)

FIGURE 5 – FEE DRAG

Exhibit 1: Investment Options			
	Index Fund	**Mutual Fund**	**Hedge Fund**
Expected return	10.00%	13.50%	19.00%
Dividend yield	1.50%	1.50%	0.00%
Standard deviation	16.00%	16.00%	16.00%
Turnover	4.00%	95.00%	200.00%
Transaction Cost	0.40%	0.40%	0.40%
Long-term gain	20.00%	20.00%	20.00%
Short-term gain	47.00%	47.00%	47.00%
Qualified dividend	20.00%	20.00%	20.00%
Management fee	0.07%	1.40%	2.00%
Performance fee	0.00%	0.00%	20.00%

Exhibit 2: Simulated Return Net of Expenses			
	Index Fund	Mutual Fund	Hedge Fund
Return gross of all expenses	10.00%	13.50%	19.00%
Transaction costs	0.02%	0.38%	0.80%
Taxes	1.64%	3.90%	5.42%
Management fee	0.07%	1.40%	2.00%
Performance fee	0.00%	0.00%	3.17%
Total expenses	1.73%	5.68%	11.39%
Return net of all expenses	8.27%	7.82%	7.61%

Source: Windham Capital.

However, there are also some potential negatives to not actually letting the fund manager run the portfolio on his or her own terms.

CONS of using 13Fs

1. **Lack of expertise in portfolio management** – The investor does not have access to the timing and portfolio trading capabilities of the manger (could also be a benefit if the manager is good at picking stocks but terrible at timing or position sizing).

2. **Inexact holdings** – Crafty hedge fund managers have some tricks to avoid revealing their holdings on 13Fs—moving positions off their book at the end of the quarter is one of them. The lack of short sales and futures reporting means that the results will differ from the hedge fund results. Managers can also get rare exemptions from reporting stocks on their 13F filings.

3. **Forty-five-day delay in reporting** – The delay in reporting will affect the portfolio in various amounts for different funds. At worst, an investor could own a position the hedge fund manager sold out of forty-five days prior. Disclosure of a new holding by some famous hedge funds, like Greenlight Capital,

can also cause a stock to move sharply before an investor has time to build a position.

4. **High-turnover strategies** – Managers who employ pairs trading or strategies that trade frequently are poor candidates for 13F replication.

5. **Arbitrage strategies** – 13F filings may show that a manager is long in a stock, when in reality he is using it in an arbitrage strategy. The short hedge will not show up on the 13F.

6. **Inconsistent manager skill** – Like any active strategy, some managers lose their desire or skill over time. How do you determine when to cut a manager from your stable of funds?

Also to note—just because you are investing alongside a great manager does not spare you from painful drawdowns. The strategy is still a long only stocks strategy that will experience similar losses to the broad stock market. However, we do tackle some hedging ideas to potentially reduce volatility and drawdowns later in this book.

Investment Styles to Avoid

An investor needs to be careful when using the government filings and understand both their strengths and weaknesses. Since there are literally thousands of hedge funds and mutual fund managers to choose from, how does one go about narrowing the list of managers? This is not an easy question to answer, and unfortunately, an intimate knowledge of the hedge fund space is a big advantage here. However, I will outline a few of the criteria to look for as well as a list/selection of managers I admire to get you started.

Resources are listed in the Appendix, and a good way to get versed in managers and their styles is to read other books on hedge fund managers. The ideal managers to follow are ones who derive a large portion of their returns from their long stock picks.

Funds to avoid include those that fit the following criteria:

Short-biased or short-only funds – Since short positions don't show up on 13F filings, it is impossible to track what hedge funds are doing with their shorts unless they disclose them publicly. (Some European exchanges report short positions, however.) Example: Kynikos Associates (Jim Chanos).

High-turnover trading – If a fund trades too much, the quarterly filings and forty-five-day delay will not accurately reflect what the fund is holding. I focus primarily on value investors in this book, which typically have lower turnover. While it is a bit fuzzy as to what level of turnover is too much, in general, the less turnover the better. Example: SAC Capital Advisors / Point72 (Steven A. Cohen).

Black box – While Medallion has certainly performed head and shoulders above almost every hedge fund in existence (after those huge 4 percent and 44 percent fees!), its investment strategies are shrouded in mystery. Is it a giant market maker, or does it invest based on the lunar cycle? Who knows? Example: Renaissance Technologies (James Simons).

Global macro and derivatives – It is hard to follow a macro manager since many trade futures, forwards, and currencies. Most commodity trading advisors (CTAS) are under this umbrella as well. A fund manager who made a ton of money on a derivatives trade, such as John Paulson did in housing, is impossible to replicate. Example: Soros Fund Management (George Soros), Winton Capital Management (David Harding).

Arbitrage – If a fund is engaging in pair trading, such as merger arbitrage, often the position will only represent half of a trade. If an investor is shorting an overvalued closed-end fund and hedging with an ETF long, that ETF will show up, but the closed-end fund will not. Example: Farallon Capital Management (Tom Steyer).

While top managers can exist at any institution—whether it is a registered investment advisor, endowment, mutual fund, or hedge fund—most of the managers I select come from hedge funds. The reasoning is simple: hedge funds offer the top compensation and tend to attract the top talent. (Now whether they earn that compensation is a separate matter. One friend describes them as a "compensation scheme masquerading as an asset class.")

Most hedge funds are also more concentrated than their mutual fund counterparts. Greater concentration suggests a higher level of confidence in stock selection since one big winner or mistake can have a major impact on returns. According to the Goldman Sachs Hedge Fund Monitor, the typical hedge fund has an average of 66 percent of its assets invested in its ten largest positions compared with 31 percent for the typical large-cap mutual fund, 22 percent for a small-cap mutual fund, 21 percent for the S&P 500, and just 3 percent for the Russell 2000 Index. (66% of assets in the top ten holdings is near identical to the amount, on average, of the funds covered later in this book.)

An academic paper published by Martijn Cremers and Antti Petajisto, "How Active is Your Fund Manager? A New Measure That Predicts Performance," demonstrates that mutual funds with a higher "active share"—the share of a portfolio that differs from its benchmark—outperform their benchmarks consistently.[6]

Before we begin with the fund manager profiles, let's take a look at some frequently asked questions to assure we are all on the same page.

Frequently Asked Questions (FAQs)

We tried to cover as many of these frequently asked questions in the text, but we get asked these so many times that they are probably worth revisiting. Here are some of the most frequently asked questions on the topic of this book:

1. **The holdings are reported forty-five days after the quarter, so you may be buying a stock the manager no longer even owns! The delay makes it impossible to follow these managers, right?**

First, remember that all of the simulated returns mentioned in this book already include the effects of using the delayed data. Also recall that if you put in enough time and careful analysis upfront, you are likely going to be tracking only funds with lower turnover in the first place.

However, in 2012, I did a study to try and quantify the effect of the forty-five-day lag. There are inherent biases no matter how you chop up the data (how many funds to include, long/short only or entire universe, include dead funds, whether to regress the returns based on turnover and AUM, etc.), but I looked at twenty funds I have been following for years on my blog. I compared rebalancing on the 13F filing date to rebalancing a portfolio at the prior quarter end (i.e., the look-ahead bias investors do not have). It shows how a portfolio constructed without the forty-five-day delay compares to a portfolio with publicly available information. Tests go back to 2000, examining the total return data with no transaction costs.

So, does the forty-five-day delay matter?

A little.

While there is wide variation across the funds (to be expected), the delay ranged anywhere from a three-percentage-point penalty for a few funds to a two-percentage-point benefit. Overall, the friction in the delay averages about 1.5 percentage points per annum (similar for both manager-weighted returns as well as equal-weighted returns). Another aside is that it doesn't matter a whole lot when you rebalance after the disclosure (i.e., there isn't much of a bounce from the filings becoming public plus or minus five days).

2. **Shorts don't show up on a manager's disclosures, so you're not really replicating their fund, right? (Ditto for futures, arbitrage situations, and undisclosed positions.)**

This is important. You are only replicating the fund's long stock positions. A firm like the Baupost Group may have most of its assets in real estate and distressed debt and only a fraction in equities. Clone portfolios will have serious tracking error in comparison to the underlying fund.

However, in many cases, the clones and hedged versions of the clones perform similarly or in some cases superiorly to the underlying fund (fees are a big reason why).

3. **Why shouldn't I just pick the top stock? Isn't that a manager's best idea?**

We have found that the top pick is usually the worst performer out of the top ten holdings, and we discuss this topic more in depth later in the book. By the time the position becomes the largest holding, it is often due to appreciation and not necessarily conviction.

4. **What funds should I track? Why can't I track the whole hedge fund universe?**

We actually think tracking the entire hedge fund universe is a great idea—for a short fund! An investor doesn't want the broad market exposure (beta) of hedge funds, which is likely to simply be S&P 500-like in nature. Investors want the alpha in hedge funds, and tracking the thousands of hedge funds, most of which are not long-term-oriented value stockpickers, is a really bad idea. You may also run the risk of being invested in stocks where there is a high concentration of funds invested in the stocks, and poses liquidation risk in case of market stress.

As far as what funds to track, I have outlined twenty funds in this book as well as dozens of funds in my first book and on my blog. Build your own list of favorites through research and, as always, through reading!

5. Can I just filter the list of stocks by market cap (or sector, momentum, etc.)?

Yes, but realize that part of the benefit of tracking these managers is their ability to "go anywhere." Also realize that any tilts to the portfolio will have the resulting impact of potentially making it less diversified or sector-biased. Some funds are inherently sector-focused, which is slightly different. Examples include healthcare-focused funds like RA, Baker Bros, Orbimed, Palo Alto, and DAFNA.

6. How do I know when to stop following a manager?

Style drift. Lost enthusiasm. Resting on laurels. A nasty divorce. Too many assets. Put in jail. Newer, younger, and hungrier managers. There are lots of reasons to move on from some managers, but the criteria can be subjective.

7. Doesn't piggybacking on these managers make them angry? Aren't you stealing their ideas?

I actually think these managers should be sending me cases of champagne! (Actually, I would prefer tequila.) Why? By definition, people following the 13Fs will be buying what these managers are selling, at some point. So far, no champagne—but I have received some nice emails.

We are now going to take a look at over twenty of my favorite managers to track for new ideas. There was no specific screening requirements to arrive at these funds; rather it is a combination of years of study coupled with quantitative as well as subjective analysis. Another fifteen fund profiles are included in the Appendix that have shorter investment track records. I will offer a very brief introduction to each manager as well as his or her backtested performance to 2000 and current holdings as of the most recent 13F filing on November 15, 2015. The profiles are in alphabetical order, but it seems fitting that we start with the top performing fund as the first profile—David Tepper's Appaloosa Management.

CHAPTER 4

APPALOOSA MANAGEMENT, DAVID TEPPER

Idea — Quotes from David Tepper & articles like it for other whole hedgies!

"The key is to wait. Sometimes the hardest thing to do is to do nothing."
— DAVID TEPPER

You would expect any management fund that takes its name from a distinctive breed of leopard-spotted horse to stand out from the crowd. Appaloosa Management does just that, in large part because of the unique and idiosyncratic investing pattern of its founder, David Tepper. Appaloosa has grown into one of the more influential and storied hedge funds, but its founder grew up in a modest neighborhood in Pittsburgh. His accountant father hit the jackpot in 1986 with a winning lottery ticket. The payoff was $30,000 per year, a windfall for the elder Tepper at the time.

These days, David Tepper earns more than that in an hour. He topped the 2014 Rich List for hedge fund manager compensation published by Institutional Investor's Alpha magazine, which estimated his 2013 earnings at $3.5 billion. It was the second year in a row that he came out number one.

What makes Tepper worth that much? The $20 billion hedge fund firm he founded in Short Hills, N.J. in 1993, Appaloosa Management, regularly churns out returns that delight his investors and wow analysts. His flagship fund, Appaloosa I, produced an estimated 29 percent net annualized gain since its launch in July 1993 through early 2014.

And Tepper is not shy about tooting his own horn: "I hope [for it] to be recognized that in the past 20 years, I arguably have the best record and therefore may be the best of this generation," he commented in an interview.

Round-faced and jovial, he projects the air of a film character actor, the simple but sincere sidekick to a leading man. His diction retains the imprint of the working-class neighborhood where he grew up, so that when he says "the markets," it comes out "dah mahkets." He once described himself as "just a regular upper-middle-class guy who happens to be a billionaire."

But while his pronunciation may not be perfect, his pronouncements and investments tend to be spot on. Wall Street views him as an investment guru worthy of emulation. These days, he has the power to move markets with a few choice words. When he was a guest on the CNBC television program *Squawk Box* in May 2013, he offered a long and detailed explanation of why he thought markets were headed higher. S&P futures had been trading lower before he spoke. By the end of the day, the S&P 500 had risen seventeen points, a bump that many attributed to a "Tepper rally."

While Tepper is closely watched for his views on equity markets, his forte is actually debt. Earlier in his career, before he was head of the high-yield desk at Goldman, Tepper worked as a finance analyst at Republic Steel Corporation of Ohio. It was there, in the midst of this financially insolvent steel corporation that Tepper learned to navigate the complex credit structure of a distressed company, a skill that would later come to define so much of his investing strategy.

By 1993, Tepper had acquired enough capital—aided by a partial cash infusion from his Goldman Sachs colleague, Jack Walton—to open Appaloosa Management to investors. The general aim of the fund was to draw on Tepper's expertise by emphasizing investments in bankruptcies and distressed situations through a 70/30 debt-equity allocation in global publicly traded markets. But beyond these loose restrictions, the fund was open to any investing opportunity, and Tepper prided himself on being sector-agnostic, event-driven, and often unorthodox.

He has a reputation for taking bets contrary to conventional market wisdom, often earning windfall returns while others were nursing losses. "The point is, markets adapt, people adapt," he once said. "Don't listen to all the crap out there."

His style relies on macro-economic and market analysis that he combines with deep and thorough research into specific investment opportunities. While he has maintained the distressed debt specialty in his strategy, he has ventured into other fields, sometimes taking a major position in a company and becoming an activist investor pushing for changes to enhance shareholder value. In recent years, some of his best returns have come from equities, leading other equity investors and analysts to closely monitor his portfolio. (For a glimpse into another famous activist, here is an article on Carl Icahn from Novus Partners.[7])

Part of Tepper's strategy is to move against the grain. Turnaround situations are his strength, such as when he bought the sovereign debt of Argentina in 1995 while most investors sought cover from the financial crisis, or similarly, when he purchased futures in South Korean currency in 1997 as most investors were pulling out of the Asian markets. Tellingly, Tepper defines his approach with statements like, "We lead the herd. The Street follows us; we don't follow the Street," and, "We're consistently inconsistent. It's one of the cornerstones of our success."

Some of his most famous bets at Appaloosa were buying debt for pennies on the dollar in big bankruptcies, including Algoma

Steel, Enron, WorldCom, and Conseco. He has also made money by buying debt in banks battered by the 2008 economic collapse as well as airlines at a time when many were facing bankruptcy. Also in late 2008, after the collapse of Lehman Brothers, he stabilized the fund by aggressively purchasing preferred shares of Wachovia and Washington Mutual for cents on the dollar. His buying spree continued, and in 2009, he picked up the preferred shares of Bank of America, the junior debt of Citigroup, and a tranche of commercial mortgage-backed securities floated by AIG. By the time the market stabilized in 2009, this concentrated allocation to financials reaped rewards beyond anything Appaloosa had ever experienced. The fund raked in a 120 percent net-of-fees return, which amounted to $7 billion to the investors and a hefty $4 billion to Tepper himself. Perhaps Tepper put it best when he said, "I am the animal at the head of the pack...I either get eaten, or I get the good grass."

Tepper often wildly shifts around sectors—he is the textbook definition of an opportunistic investor. A lot of his success has occurred due to well-timed trades like the financial sector in 2009–2011.

Maybe the best tactic when tracking Tepper is to pay attention to what he says at any given moment but to keep an even closer eye on what he does with his portfolio.

So what has he been buying recently?

FIGURE 6 – SECTOR EXPOSURE, 2000–2015

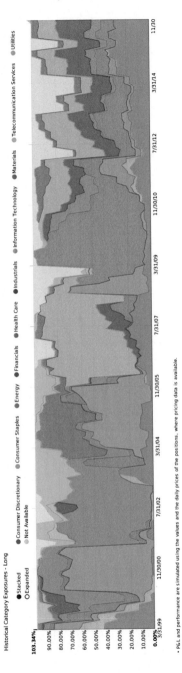

• P&L and performance are simulated using the values and the daily prices of the positions, where pricing data is available.

Source: Novus.

FIGURE 7 – 13F CURRENT HOLDINGS AS OF SEPTEMBER 30, 2015; PRICE AS OF NOVEMBER 20, 2015

Company	Symbol	Price	% of Portfolio
General Motors Co	GM	$36.34	14%
HCA Holdings Inc	HCA	$67.42	10%
Delta Air Lines Inc	DAL	$48.76	10%
NXP Semiconductors NV	NXPI	$79.77	7%
Goodyear Tire & Rubber Co	GT	$34.25	6%
Whirlpool Corp	WHR	$162.27	6%
Apple Inc	AAPL	$119.30	5%
Owens Corning	OC	$48.01	5%
Priceline Group Inc	PCLN	$1,281.53	4%
JetBlue Airways Corp	JBLU	$25.85	4%

FIGURE 8 – 13F PERFORMANCE, 2000–2014

2000-2014	Clone	S&P 500
Return	20.94%	4.31%
Volatility	26.22%	15.24%
Sharpe (1.83%)	0.73	0.16
Drawdown	-60.78%	-50.95%

Year	Clone	S&P 500	Difference
2000	38.2%	-8.2%	46.4%
2001	28.8%	-11.9%	40.7%
2002	-16.8%	-22.1%	5.3%
2003	74.6%	28.7%	45.9%
2004	46.7%	10.9%	35.8%
2005	148.0%	4.9%	143.1%
2006	32.0%	15.8%	16.2%
2007	2.8%	5.5%	-2.7%
2008	-48.0%	-37.0%	-11.0%
2009	123.2%	26.5%	96.7%
2010	23.0%	15.1%	7.9%
2011	-28.8%	2.1%	-30.9%
2012	45.3%	16.0%	29.3%
2013	52.4%	32.4%	20.0%
2014	14.4%	13.7%	0.7%

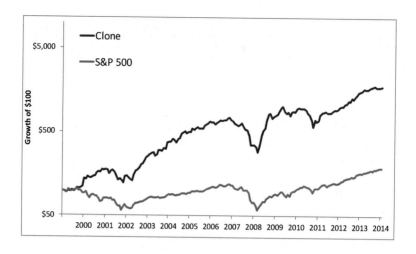

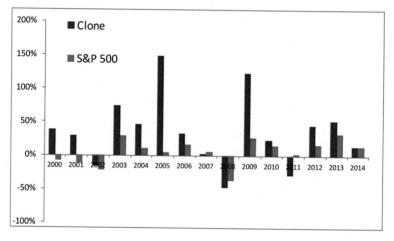

Source: AlphaClone.

CHAPTER 5

ARIEL INVESTMENTS, JOHN W. ROGERS JR.

"The problem is that most investors do not view negative returns and extreme volatility opportunistically. As self-proclaimed Buffett wannabes, we have been doing just that!"

— JOHN W. ROGERS JR.

The logo prominently displayed on Ariel Investments' homepage is of a tortoise holding up a prize cup. The reference to this Aesop fable, in which the slow and steady tortoise wins the race while the quick but overconfident hare struggles to catch up, gives some indication of Ariel's investment strategy under the direction of its founder, John W. Rogers Jr. For Rogers, a careful and methodical investment backed by diligent research always trumps a hasty move, however alluring it may seem to be. It is for good reason that his regular column in *Forbes* goes by the name of "The Patient Investor," which describes not only the information-gathering stage prior to any purchase, but also the holding time for any given investment, usually three to five years.

While he preaches patience in investing, he was decidedly impatient when it came to starting his investment company. In 1983, when he was twenty-four years old, a few years out of Princeton University and in his first job at William Blair & Company, he decided to strike out on his own. By then, he had distinguished himself by not only being the first direct-from-college hire at Blair, but also by being the first African American to join the company. Within three years, he had put together enough seed money to start Ariel Capital Management in Chicago (now called Ariel Investments), where he pursued a value investment strategy based on the methods employed by Warren Buffett. From the beginning, he has prioritized socially responsible business practices, avoiding investments in companies whose primary sources of income are derived from the production or sale of tobacco as well as those that manufacture weaponry. The fund also takes into consideration a company's stance on environmental, philanthropic, and diversity issues.

Ariel has since grown into the largest minority-owned investment company in the country, managing $11 billion in assets as of the third quarter of 2015. Rogers also gained powerful friends in Chicago, including President Barack Obama.

Today Ariel pursues its value-oriented strategy through a wide range of funds, from its original flagship fund to international and global equity funds. Some target mid-cap companies and hold forty stock positions, while others have a more concentrated portfolio of around twenty stocks, usually in companies with a market capitalization of more than $10 billion.

But in spite of their differences, they all seem to follow a similar investment strategy. Rogers constructs his portfolios using a few very specific guidelines, which he has described in various interviews over the years. He searches for companies selling at a discount of 40 percent or more relative to future earnings. He likes contrarian bets and companies or sectors that are out of favor but in which he discerns future opportunity. He bases his picks on a combination of financial research and direct contact with management, which he considers crucial.

"Getting to know the management team is the key to understanding a company and its product," he said in an interview at the 2010 Financial Analysts Seminar in Chicago. "It offers a powerful vision of the future. For those who expect to outperform, there is no substitute for a vision of the future." Because Ariel limits its investments to only a few companies each year, it is able to undertake this kind of extensive research.

In a 2012 interview, Rogers said he still maintained some positions that dated from the start of his company. "A patient and disciplined approach to investing and being cautious are the cornerstones of any successful investor," he elaborated.

Since Ariel seeks out companies that are trading at a significant discount, it sometimes invests in industries that are obscure or that fly under the radar of other funds. For instance, in an article entitled "Boring All the Way to the Bank," Rogers discusses the "glamorous returns" from a not-so-glamorous company that deals in coffins.

What is Ariel holding lately?

FIGURE 9 – 13F CURRENT HOLDINGS AS OF SEPTEMBER 30, 2015; PRICE AS OF NOVEMBER 20, 2015

Company	Symbol	Price	% of Portfolio
First American Financial Corp	FAF	$38.19	3%
Kennametal Inc	KMT	$27.57	3%
Lazard Ltd Class A	LAZ	$44.89	3%
J M Smucker Co	SJM	$122.39	3%
Interpublic Group of Companies Inc	IPG	$23.35	2%
Western Union Co	WU	$19.06	2%
International Speedway Corp Class	ISCA	$34.89	2%
Anixter International Inc	AXE	$67.01	2%
Bristow Group Inc	BRS	$29.26	2%
Laboratory Corporation of America	LH	$121.47	2%

Source: AlphaClone.

Note how much more consistent Ariel's sector bets are versus those of someone like Tepper.

FIGURE 10 – SECTOR EXPOSURE, 2000–2015

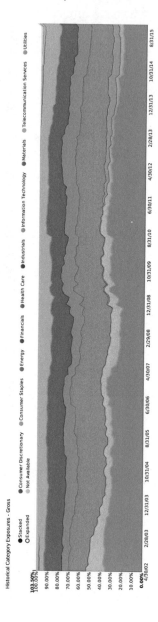

Source: Novus.

And what about performance? Ariel has outperformed by over 11 percentage points since 2000.

FIGURE 11 – 13F PERFORMANCE, 2000–2014

2000-2014	Clone	S&P 500
Return	16.38%	4.31%
Volatility	23.66%	15.24%
Sharpe (1.83%)	0.61	0.16
Drawdown	-60.63%	-50.95%

Year	Clone	S&P 500	Difference
2000	59.4%	-8.2%	67.6%
2001	14.5%	-11.9%	26.4%
2002	2.2%	-22.1%	24.3%
2003	34.6%	28.7%	5.9%
2004	20.9%	10.9%	10.0%
2005	10.6%	4.9%	5.7%
2006	14.8%	15.8%	-1.0%
2007	12.7%	5.5%	7.2%
2008	-47.4%	-37.0%	-10.4%
2009	95.6%	26.5%	69.1%
2010	23.4%	15.1%	8.3%
2011	-11.5%	2.1%	-13.6%
2012	26.0%	16.0%	10.0%
2013	42.9%	32.4%	10.5%
2014	15.3%	13.7%	1.6%

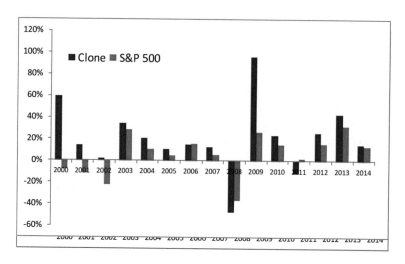

Source: AlphaClone.

CHAPTER 6

AVENIR CORPORATION, CHARLES MACKALL JR.

"We focus on what is knowable, starting with the truth that the investment process consists chiefly of purchasing future cash flows at a discount to their estimated value today."
— CHARLES MACKALL JR. IN A 2012 CLIENT LETTER[8]

Started in 1980 as a small family office in Washington, DC, Avenir has grown into a firm that oversees assets of over a billion dollars. But even though Avenir Corporation has multiplied its assets many times over, founder Charles Mackall Jr. insists that the company still maintain the personal and intimate feel of its early days. Because Mackall views the firm as a kind of family operation, he treats his clients' capital as if it were his own. Avenir Corp. has followed a philosophy of buying into companies whose stock appears to be selling at a discount but whose futures look bright, even if others on Wall Street don't see it. Like most value investors, Avenir Corp. worships at the altar of Warren Buffett and Benjamin Graham and regularly pays homage to the two icons of value investing. This means that risk is only taken when risk is justified, and otherwise, he operates with a wide margin of safety.

The firm is run by a trio of long-time executives. Co-founder Mackall, who retired from active investment management in 2013, remains chairman of the company. He spent seventeen years at NS&T Bank (Now SunTrust Banks), rising to vice president of commercial lending before leaving to form Avenir.

Heading investments today is Avenir President Peter C. Keefe, who joined the firm in 1991 after several years working in investment research with Johnston, Lemon & Co., a brokerage firm based in Washington, DC. The third partner is managing director James C. Rooney, who joined Avenir in 1998 after working in business development for two energy companies, Sonat Inc. and Columbia Energy Group.

Because Avenir believes that no one can perfectly foretell the movement of the market or the direction of interest rates all of the time, the firm opts for a "bottom-up" investment strategy that takes into account a business's fundamentals—its management team, its financial situation, and its potential growth—before purchasing any of its stock. Mackall's general philosophy is to buy a company at a significant discount to its intrinsic value. And like many funds, Avenir runs these numbers through its own independent algorithm to determine which companies present the right kinds of opportunities.

Mackall is the first to acknowledge that it's not always easy to "buy a dollar of value for fifty cents," as Benjamin Graham so clearly states it, but when you operate according to this principle, you take your time and look for excellent deals. This means that Avenir often seeks out companies that have a particular economic "franchise," which it defines as "a 'right', a 'license' or a 'privilege' that confers an economic advantage to a business permitting above-average returns on invested capital." To this end, Avenir looks for companies that tend to do well regardless of the volatility of the market. These are often businesses that specialize in goods or services that remain in strong demand even as the economy dips, such as companies that hold highly coveted leases for cell phone towers, an investment that has proven lucrative over time. The investment process at Avenir includes extensive conversations with a target company's management, during which Avenir probes for how capital is allocated. The answer Avenir wants to hear is that free cash flow is deployed in a way that enhances long-term shareholder value. That could mean anything from stock buybacks to strategic takeovers of other companies.

"If we find a great business, the only way it becomes a great investment is if management directs the marginal dollar of free cash flow to its highest-return purpose," Rooney noted in a Value Investor interview.

Avenir is not afraid of holding a stock for years or of concentrated positions. Its top fifteen holdings tend to make up as much as 80 percent of its portfolio. Once it has a major stake in a company, Avenir sometimes switches to an activist role, which can include expressing its displeasure with management's actions.

Those top holdings can represent a broad cross-section of businesses and industries. The top ten holdings recently included such names as Denny's, CarMax, and Dollar Tree.

FIGURE 12 – 13F CURRENT HOLDINGS AS OF SEPTEMBER 30, 2015; PRICE AS OF NOVEMBER 20, 2015

Company	Symbol	Price	% of Portfolio
Markel Corp	MKL	$900.47	9%
Dennys Corp	DENN	$ 9.65	9%
American Tower	AMT	$100.49	8%
American International Group Inc	AIG	$62.21	7%
Carmax Inc	KMX	$57.41	6%
Zayo Group Holdings Inc	ZAYO	$23.36	5%
Dollar Tree Inc	DLTR	$68.42	5%
Crown Holdings Inc	CCK	$51.40	5%
Popeyes Louisiana Kitchen Inc	PLKI	$54.83	5%
Microsoft Corp	MSFT	$54.19	5%

Performance has been strong, with outperformance around 10 percentage points per year since 2000 over the S&P 500.

FIGURE 13 – 13F PERFORMANCE, 2000–2014

2000-2014	Clone	S&P 500
Return	14.49%	4.31%
Volatility	21.84%	15.24%
Sharpe (1.83%)	0.58	0.16
Drawdown	-62.50%	-50.95%

Year	Clone	S&P 500	Difference
2000	13.3%	-8.2%	21.5%
2001	-4.7%	-11.9%	7.2%
2002	-11.4%	-22.1%	10.7%
2003	92.7%	28.7%	64.0%
2004	38.9%	10.9%	28.0%
2005	12.0%	4.9%	7.1%
2006	18.2%	15.8%	2.4%
2007	1.1%	5.5%	-4.4%
2008	-54.2%	-37.0%	-17.2%
2009	67.0%	26.5%	40.5%
2010	36.2%	15.1%	21.1%
2011	12.5%	2.1%	10.4%
2012	23.3%	16.0%	7.3%
2013	30.2%	32.4%	-2.2%
2014	18.1%	13.7%	4.4%

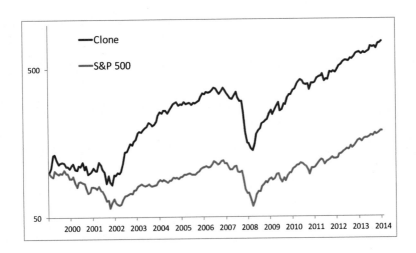

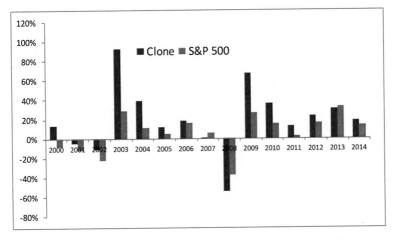

Source: AlphaClone.

CHAPTER 7

BARROW, HANLEY, MEWHINNEY & STRAUSS

Over the course of the past thirty years, Barrow, Hanley, Mewhinney & Strauss (BHMS) has proven that you do not need to take high risks in order to earn high returns. Started in 1979 in Dallas, BHMS today manages close to $70 billion in large-, mid-, and small-cap equity strategies and in fixed income strategies across the maturity spectrum. The firm continues to operate under the belief that internally-generated, fundamental research, and a bottom-up approach to investing ultimately yield the greatest results, regardless of short-term fluctuations in the market.

When it comes to equity investments, Barrow Hanley looks for strong companies across the globe that are temporarily undervalued for reasons the firm can research, identify, and understand. Specifically, it tends to invest in businesses with price/earnings and price/book ratios below the market, but with dividend yields that are substantially above the market. Barrow Hanley has always emphasized the importance of dividends.

Similarly, in the realm of fixed income, Barrow Hanley remains committed to its philosophy that securities should generate significant returns while undertaking lower risks. Barrow Hanley invests primarily in corporate bonds, mortgage securities, and alternative US government issues that are temporarily mispriced and that also promise greater yields than Treasury bonds of comparable maturity.

In addition to managing the assets of the firm, Barrow Hanley is a sub-advisor on more than thirty mutual funds, including the Vanguard Windsor II Fund, which has received much publicity in the financial press. On average, the Windsor II Fund has performed well since its inception in 1985, beating the Russell 1000 Value Index and keeping pace with the S&P 500 Index, but with less volatility.

What are some of the top holdings now?

FIGURE 14 – 13F CURRENT HOLDINGS AS OF SEPTEMBER 30, 2015; PRICE AS OF NOVEMBER 20, 2015

Company	Symbol	Price	% of Portfolio
Wells Fargo & Co	WFC	$55.82	3%
Medtronic PLC	MDT	$76.09	3%
JPMorgan Chase & Co	JPM	$67.54	3%
Philip Morris International Inc	PM	$85.99	3%
PNC Financial Services Group Inc	PNC	$95.38	3%
Pfizer Inc	PFE	$32.18	3%
Verizon Communications Inc	VZ	$45.39	2%
Johnson & Johnson	JNJ	$102.48	2%
Sanofi	SNY	$44.19	2%
Microsoft Corp	MSFT	$54.19	2%

Source: AlphaClone.

And the performance?

FIGURE 15 – 13F PERFORMANCE, 2000–2014

2000-2014	Clone	S&P 500
Return	10.63%	4.31%
Volatility	14.76%	15.24%
Sharpe (1.83%)	0.60	0.16
Drawdown	-44.38%	-50.95%

Year	Clone	S&P 500	Difference
2000	33.4%	-8.2%	41.6%
2001	-6.1%	-11.9%	5.8%
2002	-3.2%	-22.1%	18.9%
2003	33.8%	28.7%	5.1%
2004	20.2%	10.9%	9.3%
2005	19.3%	4.9%	14.4%
2006	18.3%	15.8%	2.5%
2007	11.1%	5.5%	5.6%
2008	-27.6%	-37.0%	9.4%
2009	16.4%	26.5%	-10.1%
2010	4.6%	15.1%	-10.5%
2011	4.3%	2.1%	2.2%
2012	9.2%	16.0%	-6.8%
2013	33.6%	32.4%	1.2%
2014	11.1%	13.7%	-2.6%

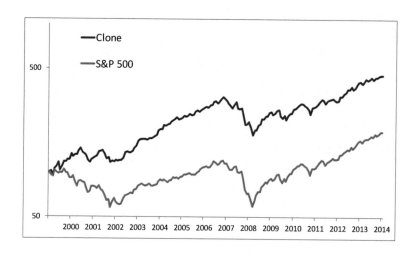

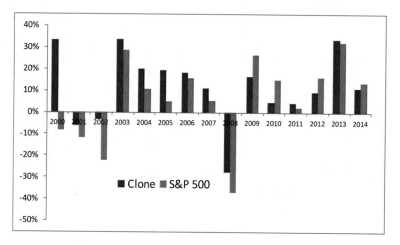

Source: AlphaClone.

CHAPTER 8

THE BAUPOST GROUP, SETH KLARMAN

"In capital markets, price is set by the most panicked seller at the end of a trading day. Value, which is determined by cash flows and assets, is not. In this environment, the chaos is so extreme, the panic selling so urgent, that there is almost no possibility that sellers are acting on superior information. Indeed, in situation after situation, it seems clear that fundamentals do not factor into their decision making at all."

— SETH KLARMAN

The Intelligent Investor, Benjamin Graham's definitive book on value investing, was selling in paperback for $12.97 on Amazon in November 2014. At the same time, *Margin of Safety*, the out-of-print investment book by Graham disciple Seth Klarman, was fetching anywhere from $2,000 to $4,597 on Amazon.

What makes the latter so valuable is not just its scarcity, but also its author. For the chance to own a bit of Klarman wisdom, adoring fans will ignore the whole concept of buying at a discount that underlies the practice of value investing. Warren Buffett, who has been called the Sage of Omaha for his value investment acumen, is in good company at the top with Seth Klarman, who has been dubbed the Sage of Boston.

Since founding Baupost Group in 1983, Klarman has grown it into a hedge fund giant managing as much as $30 billion. Its flagship fund has churned out more than 17 percent annual returns since its founding, handily beating the S&P 500 and doing it while often holding 40 percent or more of its assets in cash.

Like many value investors, Klarman likes to slowly build up concentrated bets, and he accepts long holding periods of three to five years. For example, Baupost spent three years amassing a 35-percent ownership stake in Idenix Pharmaceuticals of Cambridge, Massachusetts. When Merck & Co. announced a $4 billion takeover of Idenix in June 2014, Baupost realized nearly $1 billion in profits.

How does he do it? Klarman explained his basic philosophy to television talk-show host Charlie Rose during a 2010 interview:

"Investing is the intersection of economics and psychology," Klarman said. "The economics—the valuation of the business—is not that hard. The psychology—how much do you buy, do you buy it at this price, do you wait for a lower price, what do you do when it looks like the world might end—those things are harder. Knowing whether you stand there, buy more, or something legitimately has gone wrong and you need to sell, those are harder things. That you learn with experience. You learn by having the right psychological makeup."

Klarman went on to say that some people are born with the nerve and intuition to be great investors: "For me, it is natural. For a lot of other people it is fighting human nature." In *Margin of Safety*, Klarman credits his success to the Graham-Dodd model, claiming that one must be willing to walk away from an alluring investment should careful scrutiny reveal that the investment does not provide sufficient room for error.

Klarman hitched his natural ability to value investing after working as an intern for two years at Mutual Shares Corporation under the tutelage of Max Heine and Michael Price. A Harvard MBA, Klarman was soon recruited by one of his former professors there to run a family office. That led Klarman to launch Baupost in 1983 with $27 million, its name combining parts of the names of the families being represented. These days, its clients include Harvard University itself, along with Yale and Stanford.

Klarman has a special knack for complex transactions that often come with limited liquidity. He has purchased real estate that was acquired by the US government in the savings and loan collapse of the 1990s, dabbled in Parisian office buildings, and drilled into Russian oil companies.

Baupost made a killing in the aftermath of Bernie Madoff's massive Ponzi scheme by buying claims from victims who figured they stood little chance of fully recovering their losses. Baupost bought $230 million worth of claims for $74 million, then saw its investment more than double in value after a favorable court ruling on distribution of certain assets.

Although Klarman seems to delight in fishing for opportunity in obscure and complex deals, he is no slouch when it comes to stock picking. He runs concentrated portfolios, as is evidenced by his positions as of the third quarter of 2014. The top five represented the lion's share of his invested assets.

As a long-term investor, Klarman doesn't spend much time monitoring the daily movements of markets. His office features a desk piled high with papers, a computer, and some half-filled water bottles, but no Bloomberg terminal, the device with access to market data that traders rely upon.

Klarman runs Baupost with this same kind of deliberate planning. Rather than divide up his analysts according to specific sectors of the market—pharmaceutical, financial, oil, etc.—he assigns them to general areas of investment opportunity instead. Some focus on distressed debt while others are oriented towards post-bankruptcy equity, and still others work on spinoff and index fund deletions, and so on. This process has allowed Klarman to remain vigilant about mispriced securities, overleveraged companies, and misguided selling. And while Klarman cautions the investor against the uncertainties of the market and identifies the current economic environment as the most alarming in his lifetime, he still believes that there are real opportunities to make sound investments.

Klarman prides himself as much on not losing money as he does on making it. He has had only two negative years (1992 and 2008). (Note that Klarman invests in other assets besides stocks including real estate, bonds, and cash, and his top 10 clone would have had five down years since 2000.)

When Charlie Rose asked Klarman to name his biggest mistakes, the Sage of Boston thought for a moment, but came up empty. "I have never really screwed up a lot," Klarman said.

How many investors who have been at it for three decades can say that? Summing up his investment philosophy, he said, "I will be buying what other people are selling. I will be buying what is loathed and despised." What is Klarman buying these days? Below are his recent top-ten holdings:

FIGURE 16 – 13F CURRENT HOLDINGS AS OF SEPTEMBER 30, 2015; PRICE AS OF NOVEMBER 20, 2015

Company	Symbol	Price	% of Portfolio
Cheniere Energy Inc	LNG	$50.24	19%
ViaSat Inc	VSAT	$61.81	13%
Alcoa Inc	AA	$ 8.69	9%
Pioneer Natural Resources Co	PXD	$141.21	9%
Antero Resources Corp	AR	$21.32	6%
PayPal Holdings Inc	PYPL	$36.36	6%
PBF Energy Inc Class A	PBF	$38.27	5%
eBay Inc	EBAY	$29.06	4%
Twenty-First Century Fox Inc Class I	FOX	$30.54	3%
Atara Biotherapeutics Inc	ATRA	$33.72	3%

Source: AlphaClone.

FIGURE 17 – 13F PERFORMANCE, 2000–2014

2000-2014	Clone	S&P 500
Return	13.66%	4.31%
Volatility	26.20%	15.24%
Sharpe (1.83%)	0.45	0.16
Drawdown	-69.13%	-50.95%

Year	Clone	S&P 500	Difference
2000	9.6%	-8.2%	17.8%
2001	38.1%	-11.9%	50.0%
2002	-11.2%	-22.1%	10.9%
2003	95.1%	28.7%	66.4%
2004	19.3%	10.9%	8.4%
2005	-10.7%	4.9%	-15.6%
2006	21.9%	15.8%	6.1%
2007	-15.7%	5.5%	-21.2%
2008	-47.1%	-37.0%	-10.1%
2009	62.1%	26.5%	35.6%
2010	54.7%	15.1%	39.6%
2011	3.9%	2.1%	1.8%
2012	-7.2%	16.0%	-23.2%
2013	43.5%	32.4%	11.1%
2014	29.4%	13.7%	15.7%

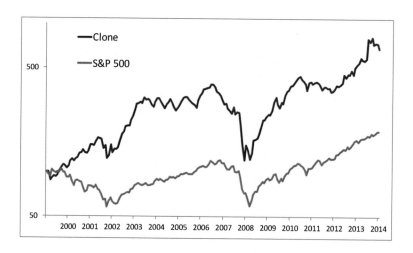

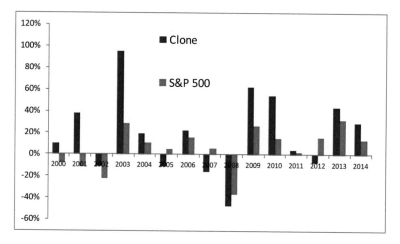

Source: AlphaClone.

CHAPTER 9

CHIEFTAIN CAPITAL MANAGEMENT / BRAVE WARRIOR, GLENN GREENBERG

"So the question is why should a decent quality or good quality business be priced to give you a 13-15 percent return when the market is priced to give you a return of about half that? Eventually somebody discovers this, somebody wakes up—it is not necessarily that the boring company with a double-digit cash flow yield has got some major trick up its sleeve; it just gets recognized as mispriced relative to the market. I would say that even though the equity market has run up quite a bit, there are still a lot of those companies around."

— GLENN GREENBERG

Glenn Greenberg knows what he likes. When he finds a company that meets his standards, he tends to go all-in. Literally.

A peak at the portfolio of Greenberg's hedge fund, Brave Warrior Advisors, for the first quarter of 2015, reveals where that mindset leads. He held just a dozen positions for an invested total of $2.7 billion. (Greenberg also tends to hold significant cash reserves of 30 percent or more). Roughly 70 percent of his invested total was tied up in his top five holdings.

Greenberg has been placing his bets this way for three decades, with enviably profitable results that have made him an icon of concentrated, long-term value investing. He has been following the same basic principles since he launched his first hedge fund, Chieftain Capital Management, in 1984, doing simple but careful analysis with a particular emphasis on cash flow in search of companies selling at a discount to future worth.

As he explained in a *Barron's* magazine interview in 1987, "Many of the companies we look at are what I refer to as geodes, stones that from the outside, to a casual observer, look to be ordinary rock, but when you crack them open and look very carefully, you see beautiful crystals."

For someone who prides himself on knowing a company's numbers, Greenberg started out mathematically challenged. The son of famed baseball player Hank Greenberg, he earned his masters at Yale University—in English. He took one math class, earned a "D," and never took another. After graduation, he went to work as a school teacher.

Someone suggested he might want to aim for a more lucrative career, so he went on to Columbia University, got his business degree, and landed a job reviewing investments for a predecessor of J.P. Morgan.

One of his first assignments was to analyze a company that had two main businesses. One was losing money. The other owned 300,000 acres of redwood forest in California. Greenberg did a simple analysis showing that the value of that land and its prized timber was worth three times the value of the entire company at the time. A light bulb flipped on and has remained lit ever since.

"That shaped my thinking," Greenberg said in a lecture at Columbia University.[9] "There are these really simply things that you don't have to be a genius to figure out. I have been doing the same thing ever since."

In his first twenty-four years, when he operated as Chieftain Capital, he produced annual returns in the 20-percent range. Then the 2008 economic collapse hit, and he lost 25 percent.

The next year, he split with his original co-founder, John Shapiro, in what has been described as a personality conflict. Shapiro re-launched under the Chieftain company name. Greenberg remained at the original business but renamed the operation Brave Warrior.

Both funds seem to remain true to the original investment strategy. Both follow a concentrated investment style, and broadly speaking, their shared investment policy follows three general rules. First, before buying equity in any company, they must feel confident that its management is strong, and once invested, ensure that it stays that way. At one point, the initial Chieftain fund went so far as to oust the CEO of Comcast once it had attained a significant stock position in the company. The second rule of thumb is that the company must fall into a certain category of business model, namely that it enjoys a local monopoly in its sector or that it demonstrates significant advantage with regard to its competition. The third rule has to do with the market valuation of the company. As Greenberg describes it, the goal is to find strong potential for growth valued at "unjustifiably" low prices. And while one must make certain projections into the future, the managers caution against adopting a time frame beyond three years, believing that anything above that horizon is simply too unpredictable to bank on.

Greenberg still pores over company reports and SEC filings, interviews company management, and does his calculations by hand on yellow legal pads.

"If you are going to be an investor," he advised Columbia students in his lecture, "you have to do the numbers yourself."

"Going for too much certainty can hold you back—there is no certainty."

Company	Symbol	Price	% of Portfolio
Valeant Pharmaceuticals International Inc	VRX	$91.00	33%
Cimpress NV	CMPR	$85.91	10%
JPMorgan Chase & Co	JPM	$67.54	10%
Microsoft Corp	MSFT	$54.19	9%
Brookfield Asset Management Inc Class A	BAM	$34.34	9%
Charles Schwab Corp	SCHW	$33.34	9%
Halliburton Co	HAL	$38.00	8%
Equinix	EQIX	$298.60	6%
Primerica Inc	PRI	$50.59	5%
Antero Resources Corp	AR	$21.32	2%

FIGURE 19 – 13F PERFORMANCE, 2000–2014

2000-2014	Clone	S&P 500
Return	13.88%	4.31%
Volatility	18.78%	15.24%
Sharpe (1.83%)	0.64	0.16
Drawdown	-60.66%	-50.95%

Year	Clone	S&P 500	Difference
2000	13.7%	-8.2%	21.9%
2001	4.6%	-11.9%	16.5%
2002	-0.7%	-22.1%	21.4%
2003	42.9%	28.7%	14.2%
2004	31.3%	10.9%	20.4%
2005	18.0%	4.9%	13.1%
2006	20.9%	15.8%	5.1%
2007	1.6%	5.5%	-3.9%
2008	-46.5%	-37.0%	-9.5%
2009	39.6%	26.5%	13.1%
2010	21.2%	15.1%	6.1%
2011	9.2%	2.1%	7.1%
2012	19.1%	16.0%	3.1%
2013	60.6%	32.4%	28.2%
2014	24.7%	13.7%	11.0%

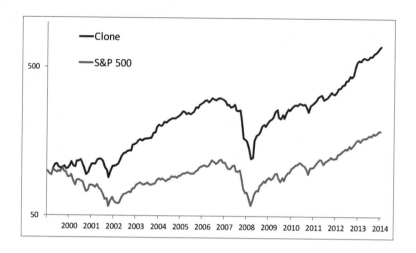

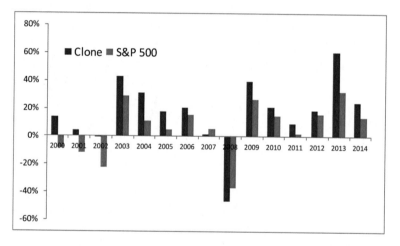

Source: AlphaClone.

CHAPTER 10

COBALT CAPITAL MANAGEMENT, WAYNE COOPERMAN

Wayne Cooperman entered the hedge fund game with an enviable pedigree. His father is Leon Cooperman, the legendary stock picker who runs Omega Advisors.

But while the younger Cooperman shares a value investing style with his father, the similarities rarely overlap in their stock selections. Wayne Cooperman has proven to be a formidable stock picker in his own right. From 1995 to 2007, his original Cobalt Capital fund posted net annualized returns of 25.7 percent after fees, versus 9.6 percent for the S&P 500.

Cobalt Capital Management casts a wide net in its stock selection. Its portfolio recently included a broad range of companies spanning everything from energy to financials to healthcare. As of the first quarter of 2014, it ran seventy-eight positions valued at $1.2 billion, without significant concentration in the top ten holdings.

Cooperman's investment philosophy is fairly straightforward. He describes what he does as searching for "above-average businesses trading at below-average prices." He uses deep fundamental analysis and makes a point of meeting and evaluating company management.

"There are two types of people who buy stocks," he says. "Those who buy them because they think they will go up and those who buy them because the value of the company is greater than the price of the stock. We have always put ourselves into the second group and have never been too good at doing things the first way."

Cooperman holds an undergraduate degree from Stanford University and an MBA from the Wharton School of Business. Before launching his hedge fund, he worked as a research analyst at Mark Asset Management, where he met Ricky Sandler, whose father, Harvey Sandler, also runs a hedge fund. Cooperman and Sandler left together to start a hedge fund called Fusion Partners in 1994. Cooperman was twenty-eight, and Sandler was twenty-five.

Sandler left the firm in 1998 and started his own hedge fund, Eminence Capital. Cooperman later changed the name of Fusion to Cobalt. He has been running the firm ever since.

Cooperman's method of stock selection relies on research into the details of a company's business. He tries to identify and understand a company's customers, its competitors, whether there are barriers to entry, and whether it has potential for expansion.

"We try to strike a balance between fully understanding the business and also spending a lot of time on valuation," he once said. "A lot of people focus primarily on the numbers and buy things that are cheap, while a lot of others just buy good businesses and don't worry as much about the numbers. We try to do both equally, and as a result, I think we make fewer mistakes."

Cooperman remains a value investor at heart. Just like his dad.

FIGURE 20 – 13F CURRENT HOLDINGS AS OF SEPTEMBER 30, 2015;
PRICE AS OF NOVEMBER 20, 2015

Company	Symbol	Price	% of Portfolio
Delta Air Lines Inc	DAL	$48.76	5%
SPDR Gold Shares	GLD	$103.09	5%
Colony Capital Inc Class A	CLNY	$20.55	4%
AerCap Holdings NV	AER	$43.24	4%
Cigna Corp	CI	$132.17	4%
Southwest Airlines Co	LUV	$47.32	3%
E*TRADE Financial Corp	ETFC	$30.25	3%
Allergan plc	AGN	$312.46	3%
Visteon Corp	VC	$118.66	3%
MGIC Investment Corp	MTG	$ 9.52	3%

Source: AlphaClone.

FIGURE 21 – 13F PERFORMANCE, 2000–2014

2000-2014	Clone	S&P 500
Return	10.99%	4.31%
Volatility	22.61%	15.24%
Sharpe (1.83%)	0.41	0.16
Drawdown	-64.49%	-50.95%

Year	Clone	S&P 500	Difference
2000	-1.2%	-8.2%	7.0%
2001	-6.7%	-11.9%	5.2%
2002	-17.6%	-22.1%	4.5%
2003	52.8%	28.7%	24.1%
2004	49.8%	10.9%	38.9%
2005	43.6%	4.9%	38.7%
2006	5.8%	15.8%	-10.0%
2007	27.9%	5.5%	22.4%
2008	-57.7%	-37.0%	-20.7%
2009	68.9%	26.5%	42.4%
2010	10.9%	15.1%	-4.2%
2011	-12.6%	2.1%	-14.7%
2012	31.4%	16.0%	15.4%
2013	33.9%	32.4%	1.5%
2014	16.1%	13.7%	2.4%

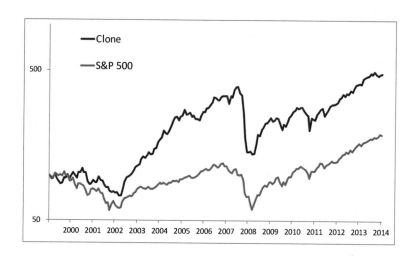

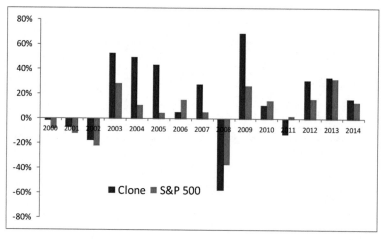

Source: AlphaClone.

CHAPTER 11

EAGLE CAPITAL MANAGEMENT, RAVENEL BOYKIN CURRY

Value investing seems to be in the genes at New York-based Eagle Capital Management, where Ravenel Boykin Curry IV not only gets his name but also his investment style from his father, Ravenel Boykin Curry III. Curry IV is the current managing partner of Eagle Capital, the hedge fund founded by his father in 1988.

The current Curry runs the firm under the same philosophy used by his dad and that has been in play at Eagle since its inception. As stated on the firm's homepage, Eagle maintains a concentrated portfolio of mainly large-cap stocks that it selects using bottom-up research. The firm is a long-only traditional asset manager that is quite different from some of the hedge funds profiled in this book that utilize shorting and leverage.

The Curry approach to investment is on display in the firm's quarterly letters to investors. In one, dated January 24, 2010, Boykin Curry IV focused on the power of long-term investing.[10] "The fact that so many investors are focused on the near-term gives those with a longer-term perspective great advantage," he wrote. As short-term investors periodically crowd into some stocks and shun others, they create market mispricings, a phenomenon that he compared to a rubber band being stretched. "A long-term investor profits when the rubber band snaps back to rationality, as it always does."

When examining fundamentals, Curry keeps an eye out for companies with beaten-down share prices that appear to have good long-term prospects. Case in point: Goldman Sachs Group, which had fallen from about $175 in early 2010 to around $95 by October of the same year. Speaking at the Value Investing Congress that October, Curry said the market was wrong and that Goldman's assets were worth closer to $150 a share than $95 and that they could go as high as $172. It took some time, and the ride was rocky, but the stock passed $150 in February 2013 and broke through $170 in July 2014.

Well-known names like Goldman are typical of Curry's picks. As of June 30, 2015, Eagle had fifty-nine positions with a total market value of approximately $25 billion. The top ten holdings represented about half of the total value and included names such as Microsoft, Oracle, and Citigroup. The number three holding: Warren Buffet's Berkshire Hathaway. Indeed, Eagle often invests in the same names as Berkshire. Meryl Whitmer, another Eagle partner, is even on the board of directors at Berkshire. Many readers will also recognize Meryl from her frequent Barron's Roundtable appearances, on which she has been featured since 1999.

While Eagle operates out of offices in New York and Boykin Curry is a fixture on the city's social and non-profit scene, his family roots are in Greenwood, S.C. His grandfather, Ravenel Boykin Curry, Jr., who died in 2012 at the age of ninety-six, owned and operated Citizens Trust Co. in Greenwood. Ravenel Boykin Curry III moved to New York and launched Eagle in 1988.

Boykin Curry IV holds an undergraduate degree in economics from Yale University and an MBA from Harvard Business School. He managed investments for Morgan Stanley Asset Management and hedge fund Kingdon Capital before joining his father at Eagle. Eagle has a solid record of outperforming the S&P 500. As of early 2014, it had a cumulative return since inception of 2,031 percent, versus 634 percent for the S&P 500.

FIGURE 22 – 13F CURRENT HOLDINGS AS OF SEPTEMBER 30, 2015; PRICE AS OF NOVEMBER 20, 2015

Company	Symbol	Price	% of Portfolio
Oracle Corp	ORCL	$39.34	7%
Berkshire Hathaway Inc Class B	BRK.B	$136.63	6%
Microsoft Corp	MSFT	$54.19	6%
Liberty Global PLC Class C	LBTYK	$40.86	6%
Citigroup Inc	C	$54.75	5%
Aon PLC Class A	AON	$94.86	5%
ALPHABET INC	GOOG	$ 0.00	5%
Amazon.com Inc	AMZN	$668.45	5%
Ecolab Inc	ECL	$118.13	4%
UnitedHealth Group Inc	UNH	$112.97	4%

Source: AlphaClone.

FIGURE 23 – 13F PERFORMANCE, 2000–2014

2000-2014	Clone	S&P 500
Return	12.74%	4.31%
Volatility	15.93%	15.24%
Sharpe (1.83%)	0.68	0.16
Drawdown	-44.21%	-50.95%

Year	Clone	S&P 500	Difference
2000	58.5%	-8.2%	66.7%
2001	0.8%	-11.9%	12.7%
2002	-2.3%	-22.1%	19.8%
2003	31.4%	28.7%	2.7%
2004	15.8%	10.9%	4.9%
2005	5.2%	4.9%	0.3%
2006	13.3%	15.8%	-2.5%
2007	6.5%	5.5%	1.0%
2008	-28.5%	-37.0%	8.5%
2009	14.1%	26.5%	-12.4%
2010	24.0%	15.1%	8.9%
2011	7.1%	2.1%	5.0%
2012	22.0%	16.0%	6.0%
2013	36.3%	32.4%	3.9%
2014	11.1%	13.7%	-2.6%

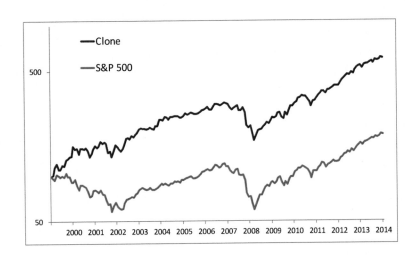

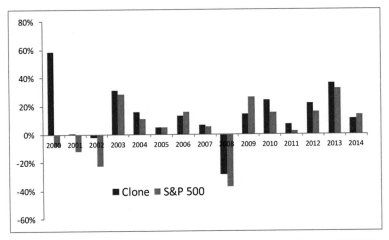

Source: AlphaClone.

CHAPTER 12

EMINENCE CAPITAL LLC, RICKY SANDLER

"Volatility can be a friend of the value investor — it provides more situations where stocks significantly diverge from their intrinsic value and can allow us to turn our capital faster."

— RICKY SANDLER

By the age of twenty-five, Ricky Sandler had co-founded the investment fund Fusion Partners with his colleague, Wayne Cooperman. In a mere four years, their initial seed money of $28 million had mushroomed into $350 million with a net annual return of 31 percent. The fund split amicably in 1998, and Sandler quickly set up Eminence Capital to take its place. Over the last thirteen years, Eminence has achieved close to 13 percent net annual compounded returns, with only one down year on record: 19 percent in 2008. While he maintains a similar investment strategy to the Fusion Partners fund, Sandler has revised certain aspects of his investment philosophy, namely in relation to value pricing, as well as the fund's long-short position ratio.

When looking for long ideas, Eminence seeks discounts that may be caused by a number of different factors. In particular, it looks for three different types of opportunities. First, it is on the lookout for good businesses that may suffer because they are part of a temporarily neglected industry. Second, they scout opportunities in otherwise strong companies that have recently reported disappointing short-term earnings, especially if the company's long-term value remains unimpaired. Finally, Eminence searches for good companies that may fly under other analysts' radars, often because their attention is focused on other industries or because the business is in the process of undergoing a special situation, such as a spin-off.

Sandler upholds the philosophy that entry price is a crucial factor in determining value. But whereas he may have once avoided investments in less-than-stellar businesses, he is now open to opportunities that even mediocre businesses may provide. As he explains it, Sandler wants to buy "a great business at a reasonable price" or "a reasonable business at a great price." Additionally, Sandler looks for stocks that fall into a category that he calls, "old research, new events," meaning that the company has already proven its worth according to Eminence's independent research, but is, perhaps, experiencing a momentary lapse in value. But unlike many others in the value game, Sandler is willing to invest at a much smaller perceived discount if he believes he is buying a high-quality company with solid future potential.

"I'm probably more willing to pay up for quality than other value investors," Sandler said in an interview with *Value Investor Insight*.[11] "Some of my investor friends often tell me my ideas are too high quality for them."

He likes to hold major positions for eighteen months to two years, but he closely monitors volatility in search of both buy and sell opportunities. When it comes to shorting stock, Eminence embraces a philosophy that shorting offers a totally different perspective on the market and one that lends the wise investor excellent investment opportunities. Put in its most basic terms, Sandler believes that shorting introduces into one's investment perspective some degree of skepticism, which often exposes value traps that can be triggered by creative accounting or unsustainably optimistic management projections. Although at one time, Sandler built the fund's short positions on individual stocks, now he also makes use of indices to achieve the same end.

While Eminence Capital is classified as a long-short equity fund, Sandler sometimes adopts an activist stance, as he did during the merger battle between Jos. A. Bank and Men's Wearhouse. Eminence owned a significant stake in both companies, and Sandler aggressively advanced its interests with a series of comments and letters to the boards as the contentious merger talks dragged on. When a deal agreeable (and profitable) to Sandler finally emerged in April 2014, he issued a press release praising the two sides.

Sandler also runs a less concentrated portfolio than some of his value investing peers.

FIGURE 24 – 13F CURRENT HOLDINGS AS OF SEPTEMBER 30, 2015; PRICE AS OF NOVEMBER 20, 2015

Company	Symbol	Price	% of Portfolio
Autodesk Inc	ADSK	$60.55	5%
Baidu Class A	BIDU	$206.69	4%
GNC Holdings Inc Class A	GNC	$29.08	3%
Keurig Green Mountain Inc	GMCR	$47.44	3%
TripAdvisor Inc	TRIP	$84.98	3%
Genpact Ltd	G	$25.31	3%
Michael Kors Holdings Ltd	KORS	$41.13	3%
Alphabet Inc Class C	GOOG	$756.60	3%
Men's Wearhouse Inc	MW	$19.77	3%
Zynga Inc Class A	ZNGA	$ 2.54	3%

Source: AlphaClone.

FIGURE 25 – 13F PERFORMANCE, 2000–2014

2000-2014	Clone	S&P 500
Return	12.18%	4.31%
Volatility	16.80%	15.24%
Sharpe (1.83%)	0.62	0.16
Drawdown	-41.95%	-50.95%

Year	Clone	S&P 500	Difference
2000	23.8%	-8.2%	32.0%
2001	5.7%	-11.9%	17.6%
2002	-18.3%	-22.1%	3.8%
2003	50.6%	28.7%	21.9%
2004	29.9%	10.9%	19.0%
2005	8.7%	4.9%	3.8%
2006	19.6%	15.8%	3.8%
2007	7.1%	5.5%	1.6%
2008	-26.7%	-37.0%	10.3%
2009	23.5%	26.5%	-3.0%
2010	21.3%	15.1%	6.2%
2011	-1.0%	2.1%	-3.1%
2012	22.1%	16.0%	6.1%
2013	40.2%	32.4%	7.8%
2014	7.7%	13.7%	-6.0%

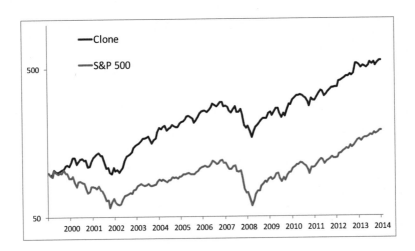

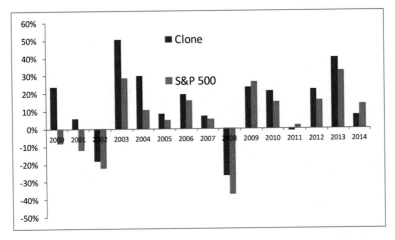

Source: AlphaClone.

CHAPTER 13

GARDNER, RUSSO, AND GARDNER

"Ninety-five percent of the world does not live in the United States. Figure out a way to make investments that recognize the promise of that 95 percent of the world. That happens all the time."

— TOM RUSSO

Meet the Joe Lunchbucket of international investing. His name is Tom Russo, and he has an appetite for beer and frozen pizza, cigarettes and chocolate candy, all on a global scale. Russo has built a reputation as a savvy long-term investor by buying and holding companies with established international brands in alcohol, tobacco, and food. He also dabbles in media stocks and has a particular fondness for Warren Buffett, whose Berkshire Hathaway has long been a major component of Russo's portfolio.

A partner at Gardner Russo & Gardner in Lancaster, Pennsylvania, a firm that manages more than $10 billion, Russo runs a concentrated portfolio guided by the principles of long-term value investing and informed by a world view that sees profit in businesses capable of growing basic consumer brands globally. You won't find trendy companies like Facebook or Twitter in his portfolio. Instead, he buys companies like Nestle, Heineken, and Phillip Morris. He has a special fondness for businesses that show promise in emerging markets. When he finds a company he likes, he buys big and holds for years.

Commenting on his investment picks a few years ago, he noted, "We often find ourselves out of step, invested in things that are out of fashion." Out of step, however, doesn't mean out of the money. Russo's signature Temper Vic Partners fund gained 12.9 percent annualized from inception in 1990 to September 30, 2013.

Many of his picks are European companies that have a history of expanding beyond their national borders, sometimes by necessity in their search for new customers. Nestle, for example, is based in Switzerland, a country with eight million people. Dutch brewer Heineken comes from the Netherlands, whose population is about sixteen million.

He likes companies that are family controlled, a characteristic that often scares off other investors concerned that such companies will be more interested in enriching the clan than catering to investors. As a result, those companies often trade at discount compared to similar companies without the family ties. Russo searches for well-run, family controlled companies that he can buy for as little as half of what he feels they are actually worth based on their future prospects. He once estimated that 60 percent of his investments are in companies still run by founding families.

The other quality he seeks is a business capable of absorbing short-term financial challenges as it tries to capture new markets and customers. "Companies have to have the capacity to suffer when they want to expand," Russo says.

A native of Wisconsin, Russo graduated from Dartmouth College, earned his law and business degrees at Stanford University, and then landed a job at Sequoia Fund in 1984. Much of his investment style derives from his time at Sequoia, another value investing asset manager that specialized in food, beverages, tobacco, and media.

In 1989, he moved from Sequoia in New York to Lancaster, Pennsylvania, where he joined Eugene Gardner and Eugene Gardner, Jr., to form Gardner Russo & Gardner.

Russo has been buying and holding companies with international consumer brands ever since and churning out regular profits by being patient and not expecting the companies he picks to produce immediate windfalls but rather to plow profits back into expansion that can produce future gains.

"The key to success in investing is low expectations," he once said. "My goal is to find businesses I can hold onto forever."

FIGURE 26 – 13F CURRENT HOLDINGS AS OF SEPTEMBER 30, 2015; PRICE AS OF NOVEMBER 20, 2015

Company	Symbol	Price	% of Portfolio
Nestle Series B	NSRGY	$74.60	11%
Berkshire Hathaway Inc Class A	BRK.A	$204,600.00	9%
MasterCard Inc Class A	MA	$99.50	8%
Philip Morris International Inc	PM	$85.99	8%
Heineken Holding NV	HKHHF	$79.00	7%
Wells Fargo & Co	WFC	$55.82	7%
CIE FINANCIERE RICHEMONT AG ZL	CFRHF	$ 0.00	6%
SABMiller PLC	SBMRF	$61.61	6%
Unilever	UN	$44.58	5%
Pernod Ricard SA	PDRDF	$114.64	5%

Source: AlphaClone.

FIGURE 27 – 13F PERFORMANCE, 2000–2014

2000-2014	Clone	S&P 500
Return	10.96%	4.31%
Volatility	14.43%	15.24%
Sharpe (1.83%)	0.63	0.16
Drawdown	-44.62%	-50.95%

Year	Clone	S&P 500	Difference
2000	38.6%	-8.2%	46.8%
2001	2.7%	-11.9%	14.6%
2002	-1.1%	-22.1%	21.0%
2003	23.8%	28.7%	-4.9%
2004	6.4%	10.9%	-4.5%
2005	1.9%	4.9%	-3.0%
2006	24.7%	15.8%	8.9%
2007	7.7%	5.5%	2.2%
2008	-29.3%	-37.0%	7.7%
2009	25.3%	26.5%	-1.2%
2010	20.7%	15.1%	5.6%
2011	4.0%	2.1%	1.9%
2012	27.1%	16.0%	11.1%
2013	24.4%	32.4%	-8.0%
2014	6.7%	13.7%	-7.0%

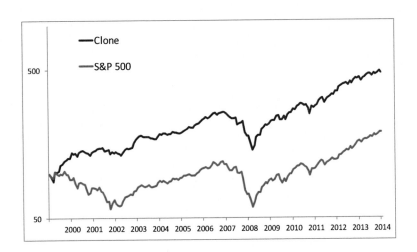

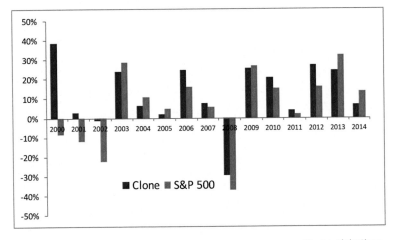

Source: AlphaClone.

CHAPTER **14**

GREENLIGHT CAPITAL, DAVID EINHORN

"What I like is solving the puzzles. I think that what you are dealing with here is incomplete information. You've got little bits of things. You have facts. You have analysis. You have numbers. You have people's motivations. And you try to put this together into a puzzle or decode the puzzle in a way that allows you to have a way better than average opportunity to do well if you solve the puzzle correctly, and that's the best part of the business."

— DAVID EINHORN

As an ace poker player (he has won millions in high-stakes tournaments and donated his take to charity), David Einhorn knows how to read the table—when to go all in on a hand he trusts and when to bet against a bluffing opponent. He plays the stock market in much the same way.

Einhorn's multi-billion dollar Greenlight Capital runs a concentrated portfolio heavily skewed toward his top positions, and the top six accounted for more than half of invested positions in the first quarter of 2015, according to his SEC filings. But for someone with that much money riding on companies he likes, Einhorn tends to get much more attention for the companies he hates.

An Einhorn short generates major headlines and can have the power to move a stock's price. Companies on the receiving end of one of his short plays are said to be "Einhorned," a term he joked about in a 2012 conference with the line, "Apparently now I'm a verb."

He was once investigated by the SEC for market manipulation after discussing his short position against finance firm Allied Capital; his comments at a 2002 conference about his short generated so much activity in the stock that trading was temporarily suspended.

It took years to resolve, but Einhorn was eventually vindicated and the company taken to task by the SEC. Allied was subsequently bought out and taken private, and Einhorn wrote a book about the experience, *Fooling Some of the People Some of the Time.*

There have been a number of other high-profile campaigns against companies since then. He argued that Lehman Brothers was using suspicious accounting and overly risky practices; the company collapsed in 2008 during the economic meltdown. He presented a 100-page attack on Green Mountain Coffee Roasters in 2012 and delivered a sixty-six-page presentation in 2014 explaining his short against Athena Health. That presentation concluded with a vintage line from Einhorn: "We believe that there are serious risks to this business model that are being mostly ignored by bullish investors and sell-side analysts." [12]

That comment belies the ferocity with which Einhorn often pursues his prey. A profile in the *New York Daily News* quoted an unnamed source in describing how Einhorn works: "He does deals where he rips your face off. If he had a fin, he'd be swimming in the ocean."

While it may be uncomfortable to be on the receiving end of an Einhorn short, it can be quite profitable to place money with him. He doesn't always come out on top, but the thesis behind each investment—long or short—is based on such deep research and intensive analysis that even other hedge fund managers are impressed. One hedge fund manager described what Einhorn does as "extraordinarily detailed work."

A graduate of Cornell University with a degree in government, Einhorn interned with the SEC and considered joining the CIA, but wound up taking a job at investment bank Donaldson, Lufkin and Jenrette (which was later bought out by Credit Suisse). Two years later, he left for a job at hedge fund Siegler Collery & Co., and in 1996 launched Greenlight with a colleague from that firm.

Greenlight has since grown from less than $1 million in assets to more than $10 billion, while Einhorn himself has become a billionaire and earned a reputation as a masterful short seller. That reputation tends to overlook his other skill as a long investor running a highly concentrated portfolio. However, his story is one that is really about two periods—2000-2006, and 2007-2015. From 2000 – 2006, Einhorn beat the S&P500 every single year, on average by a whopping 27 percentage points per year! Since then? On average his 13F long picks have trailed the S&P 500 by about 4 percentage points a year. This trend generates a classic question for investors, "When do I stop following a manager?" There are no easy answers, although we did cover a few ideas in the FAQ.

FIGURE 28 – 13F CURRENT HOLDINGS AS OF SEPTEMBER 30, 2015; PRICE AS OF NOVEMBER 20, 2015

Company	Symbol	Price	% of Portfolio
Apple Inc	AAPL	$119.30	21%
General Motors Co	GM	$36.34	8%
Michael Kors Holdings Ltd	KORS	$41.13	5%
Chicago Bridge & Iron Company NV	CBI	$41.92	5%
CONSOL Energy Inc	CNX	$ 7.87	5%
AerCap Holdings NV	AER	$43.24	5%
UIL Holdings Corp	UIL	$48.58	5%
Time Warner Inc	TWX	$70.72	5%
Green Brick Partners Inc	GRBK	$ 7.46	4%
Micron Technology Inc	MU	$15.43	3%

Source: AlphaClone.

FIGURE 29 − 13F PERFORMANCE, 2000−2014

2000-2014	Clone	S&P 500
Return	13.12%	4.31%
Volatility	21.54%	15.24%
Sharpe (1.83%)	0.52	0.16
Drawdown	-57.39%	-50.95%

Year	Clone	S&P 500	Difference
2000	48.6%	-8.2%	56.8%
2001	18.7%	-11.9%	30.6%
2002	-20.0%	-22.1%	2.1%
2003	75.6%	28.7%	46.9%
2004	44.6%	10.9%	33.7%
2005	21.7%	4.9%	16.8%
2006	17.9%	15.8%	2.1%
2007	-13.0%	5.5%	-18.5%
2008	-39.1%	-37.0%	-2.1%
2009	27.2%	26.5%	0.7%
2010	17.7%	15.1%	2.6%
2011	-6.9%	2.1%	-9.0%
2012	11.4%	16.0%	-4.6%
2013	35.6%	32.4%	3.2%
2014	10.9%	13.7%	-2.8%

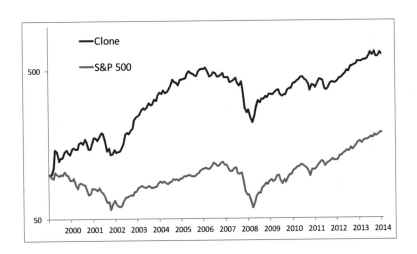

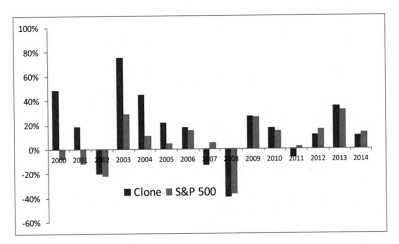

Source: AlphaClone.

CHAPTER 15

LSV ASSET MANAGEMENT, JOSEF LAKONISHOK

"I never could understand why anybody would buy a company and pay huge multiples for it. You need a lot of luck to be able to justify such prices, because markets are competitive. If you have a good product, you will attract competition."

— JOSEF LAKONISHOK

Josef Lakonishok knows what you're thinking. He knows how and why you invest, why you pay too much for stocks going nowhere, why you hang onto losers, why you ignore undervalued gems. And he profits by your psychological weaknesses.

A university professor turned investment advisor, Lakonishok took his financial and behavioral research, put it together with that of two other professors, and formed LSV Asset Management in 1994, a quantitative value equity shop that has grown into an $83 billion behemoth.

Like other value investors, Lakonishok likes companies toiling in the shadow of hot momentum stocks. Where he differs is how he goes about sourcing his picks. Lakonishok relies on a series of computer models that combine theories of investment behavior with more traditional screens for spotting companies whose cheap current prices belie their abilities to produce future profits.

The LSV website lays out its thinking: "The basic premise on which our investment philosophy is based is that superior results can be achieved by systematically exploiting the judgmental biases and behavioral weaknesses that influence the decisions of many investors."

Lakonishok is so wedded to his quantitative approach that he sees little need to do the more mundane legwork that many of his value investing peers practice. If his screens tell him a company is worth owning, he sees no reason to pay the business a visit.

As he once said, "We don't visit companies, and we don't talk to analysts."

The other thing he doesn't do is run a highly concentrated portfolio. As of the first quarter of 2014, LSV held 905 positions, and while financials represented the largest sector at 25 percent, there were also significant holdings in technology, energy, services, and healthcare.

Lakonishok spent years doing academic research into behavioral finance. He concluded that investors tend to rely too much on the past when trying to predict the future, they overpay for good companies, they ignore statistics, and they develop mindsets about companies that affect their decisions. By playing off those tendencies, LSV avoids overpriced companies and trolls for promising bargains:

"I always believed that if people are getting too excited about a performance of a company that is doing well for a prolonged time period, as did Cisco, Microsoft, etc., investors extrapolate past performance too far into the future and push prices up too high. Eventually these companies will disappoint investors."

It isn't a foolproof system, but it is effective enough to have attracted a loyal following to Lakonishok's theories. In his 2001 book, *Investment Titans - Investment Insights from the Minds That Move Wall Street,* Jonathan Burton selected Lakonishok as one of nine profiled market gurus. Interestingly, Lakonishok never worked on Wall Street, moving directly from the classroom to his firm.

Lakonishok holds BA and MBA degrees from Tel Aviv University, as well as an MS and PhD in Business Administration from Cornell University. He has held several academic positions, winding up as the William G. Karnes Professor of Finance at the College of Commerce & Business Administration at the University of Illinois at Urbana-Champaign.

He published more than eighty articles, conducted research in finance and trading, and received numerous awards for his academic work. One of those award-winning papers, "Contrarian Investment, Extrapolation, and Risk," written with Harvard Economics professor Dr. Andrei Shleifer and University of Chicago finance professor Robert Vishny, led to the three of them forming LSV in 1994. Shleifer and Vishny have since retired from the firm, leaving Lakonishok to run things.

"We are quantitative value money managers. There are more and more quantitative money managers today, but I think that when we started, you didn't really have that many active value money managers."

So far, Lakonishok has shown no interest in retiring, continuing to delight in probing the minds of conventional investors and profit by investing contrary to them.

Company	Symbol	Price	% of Portfolio
Pfizer Inc	PFE	$32.18	3%
Johnson & Johnson	JNJ	$102.48	3%
AT&T Inc	T	$33.66	2%
JPMorgan Chase & Co	JPM	$67.54	2%
Cisco Systems Inc	CSCO	$27.57	2%
Exxon Mobil Corp	XOM	$79.79	2%
Intel Corp	INTC	$34.66	2%
Citigroup Inc	C	$54.75	1%
Verizon Communications Inc	VZ	$45.39	1%
Northrop Grumman Corp	NOC	$189.48	1%

Source: AlphaClone.

FIGURE 31 – 13F PERFORMANCE, 2000–2014

2000-2014	Clone	S&P 500
Return	9.51%	4.31%
Volatility	16.23%	15.24%
Sharpe (1.83%)	0.47	0.16
Drawdown	-51.29%	-50.95%

Year	Clone	S&P 500	Difference
2000	10.9%	-8.2%	19.1%
2001	-6.5%	-11.9%	5.4%
2002	-11.0%	-22.1%	11.1%
2003	37.0%	28.7%	8.3%
2004	26.4%	10.9%	15.5%
2005	18.4%	4.9%	13.5%
2006	32.5%	15.8%	16.7%
2007	6.8%	5.5%	1.3%
2008	-25.2%	-37.0%	11.8%
2009	5.2%	26.5%	-21.3%
2010	10.8%	15.1%	-4.3%
2011	-1.5%	2.1%	-3.6%
2012	15.8%	16.0%	-0.2%
2013	29.4%	32.4%	-3.0%
2014	13.2%	13.7%	-0.5%

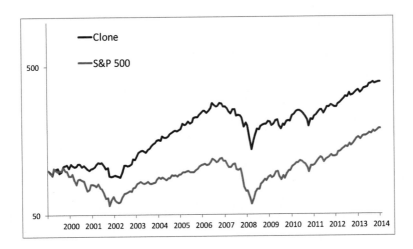

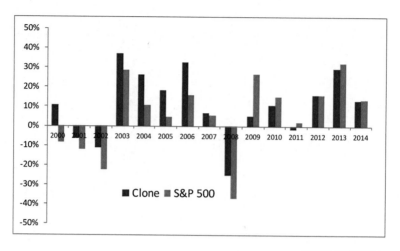

Source: AlphaClone.

CHAPTER 16

PAR CAPITAL MANAGEMENT, PAUL A. REEDER III

With a new MBA in hand from the MIT Sloan School of Management in Boston, Paul A. Reeder III went shopping for a job. He found one at Loomis Sayles & Company, the mutual fund firm based in Boston, where he became a highly regarded airline analyst. Indeed, his observations were so valuable that Reeder decided he could parlay it into his own fund company.

In 1990 he founded PAR Capital Management in Boston, an equity hedge fund that specialized in airlines and the travel industry and practiced a form of value investing. In 1997, Edward L. Shapiro, a vice president of Boston-based hedge fund sponsor Wellington Management, came aboard as a partner and portfolio manager, bringing complimentary experience vetting airline and travel companies.

The duo has been flying high ever since. PAR is now a $3 billion fund manager and has branched out to gaming, hospitality, healthcare, and technology. But airlines, travel, and businesses related to that field are still the duo's forte.

Tagging along with PAR's stock picks can be very rewarding.

An article posted by The Motley Fool in September 2011 concluded that investing in PAR's top ten positions at the time they were disclosed would have gained 231 percent since 2000, versus a loss of 1 percent for the S&P 500.

PAR runs dynamic portfolios that include as many as seventy positions and frequent changes. The investment style is summed up on the firm's homepage: "Our philosophy is based on the belief that long-term investment success can be achieved through narrowly focused and rigorous fundamental research, disciplined portfolio management, and the alignment of incentives between manager and client."

When PAR becomes one of the largest shareholders in a company, it adopts an activist role, taking board seats and pressing for changes. Much of the dirty work during activist roles is done by Shapiro, who has been a board member of numerous companies in the PAR portfolio over the years, including US Airways, America West Airlines, and LodgeNet Interactive Corp.

These days, PAR is so closely watched that its actions can move stock prices. In 2013, PAR sold a third of its nearly 25 million shares in Orbitz Worldwide Inc., saying it was diversifying its portfolio. PAR at the time was one of the largest shareholders in Orbitz, with a 23-percent stake. When news of the PAR sale broke, the stock sank 11.8 percent in one day.

Warren Buffett said, "The worst sort of business is one that grows rapidly, requires significant capital to engender the growth, and then earns little or no money. Think airlines." Despite this, PAR continues to be a major player in airline stocks and the travel sector—its filing for March 2015 included significant holdings in Alaska Air Group, Delta Air Lines, Southwest Airlines, and United Airlines. It was also was a major player in new online travel booking and review companies, including TripAdvisor Inc. and Expedia Inc. It also holds gaming stocks and leisure companies, including Global Eagle Entertainment and Churchill Downs. Of course, not all of PAR's bets pan out. But its record of success has made others consider it worthy of following, especially when the play is related to airlines or travel. (For more information and analysis of PAR, view this Novus analysis of the fund.[13])

FIGURE 32 – 13F CURRENT HOLDINGS AS OF SEPTEMBER 30, 2015; PRICE AS OF NOVEMBER 20, 2015

Company	Symbol	Price	% of Portfolio
Delta Air Lines Inc	DAL	$48.76	14%
Expedia Inc	EXPE	$126.25	9%
Alaska Air Group Inc	ALK	$81.86	8%
Global Eagle Entertainment Inc	ENT	$10.57	7%
United Continental Holdings Inc	UAL	$58.81	6%
Southwest Airlines Co	LUV	$47.32	5%
Churchill Downs Inc	CHDN	$145.81	4%
Priceline Group Inc	PCLN	$1,281.53	3%
Boyd Gaming Corp	BYD	$20.17	3%
Gaming and Leisure Properties	GLPI	$27.43	3%

Source: AlphaClone.

FIGURE 33 – 13F PERFORMANCE, 2000–2014

2000-2014	Clone	S&P 500
Return	15.38%	4.31%
Volatility	27.87%	15.24%
Sharpe (1.83%)	0.49	0.16
Drawdown	-55.20%	-50.95%

Year	Clone	S&P 500	Difference
2000	11.0%	-8.2%	19.2%
2001	-17.4%	-11.9%	-5.5%
2002	-12.3%	-22.1%	9.8%
2003	65.6%	28.7%	36.9%
2004	10.4%	10.9%	-0.5%
2005	15.9%	4.9%	11.0%
2006	40.8%	15.8%	25.0%
2007	8.1%	5.5%	2.6%
2008	-38.3%	-37.0%	-1.3%
2009	70.1%	26.5%	43.6%
2010	14.4%	15.1%	-0.7%
2011	-2.5%	2.1%	-4.6%
2012	29.6%	16.0%	13.6%
2013	75.4%	32.4%	43.0%
2014	24.2%	13.7%	10.5%

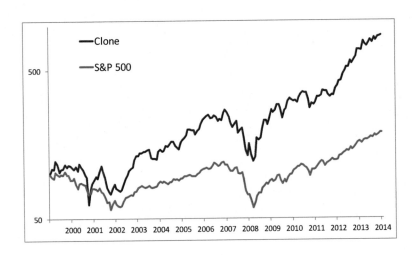

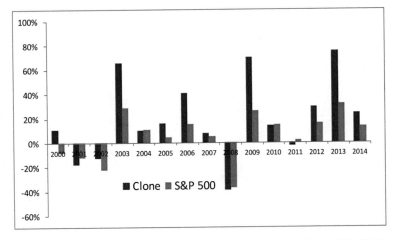

Source: AlphaClone.

CHAPTER 17

RAIFF PARTNERS, ROBERT RAIFF

Robert Raiff doesn't mind betting a sizable chunk of his portfolio on a single position, regardless of how popular or unpopular a particular company is at the time. As a value investor interested in companies that generate solid cash flow, he likes to concentrate his Raiff Partners Inc. on what he sees as his best ideas.

Case in point: Apple Inc. Raiff loved the company in 2011 and 2012 and stuffed his portfolio with shares. As of the third quarter of 2012, Apple represented a quarter of his holdings.

But Raiff is also quick to pare his position when he thinks a stock has hit a peak. In the case of Apple, he sold off half of his shares by the end of 2012.

By hedge fund standards, Raiff runs a fairly small book. His invested long equity assets were valued at $87 million as of the second quarter of 2015. But as he said when he launched his fund in 1995, he never meant to be one of the mega-managers, intending to run no more than $500 million at any one time.

Raiff started out as a research analyst and has parlayed that skill into direct investment. After obtaining his undergraduate degree from Brown University and his MBA from Columbia University, he went to work for investment research and securities firm C.J. Lawrence, where he earned a reputation as a skillful value investing stock picker for the firm's clients.

As he explained in an interview, he used a fairly straightforward approach to making stock picks. "I look for stocks trading at low multiples of cash flow," he said.

After 10 years at C.J. Lawrence, he moved to Soros Fund Management, the storied hedge fund run by George Soros, where he was tasked with investing in stocks around the world.

He stayed with Soros for four years before leaving in 1995 to launch his own fund, Raiff Partners, in New York. The original idea was to apply his skills at fundamental analysis and value-style investment to smaller stocks.

But while he has maintained his value approach, he has expanded the horizon of companies he picks to some of the largest and most widely traded companies. He has also been a significant player in tech stocks, a departure from his original field of expertise in retail. In addition to Apple, he has also been an investor in Google, Intel, and AT&T.

As of the third quarter of 2015, he held thirty-seven positions, and Apple still represented his largest single holding at nearly 33 percent of his portfolio.

Joining Apple in the top ten were a variety of companies, including Pfizer and Walt Disney. As a group, those top ten accounted for about 74 percent of the portfolio. Technology was his favorite sector (33 percent).

Most of Raiff's investments these days seem to be with larger companies that are often favored by many other hedge funds, including his old boss, Soros.

FIGURE 34 – 13F CURRENT HOLDINGS AS OF SEPTEMBER 30, 2015; PRICE AS OF NOVEMBER 20, 2015

Company	Symbol	Price	% of Portfolio
Apple Inc	AAPL	$119.30	33%
Ranger Equity Bear	HDGE	$10.47	12%
J C Penney Company Inc	JCP	$ 7.79	11%
Ares Capital Corp	ARCC	$15.61	10%
ACE Ltd	ACE	$116.48	9%
General Electric Co	GE	$30.66	9%
American Eagle Outfitters Inc	AEO	$15.75	6%
Apollo Investment Corp	AINV	$ 6.07	4%
TransUnion	TRU	$25.75	2%
KLX Inc	KLXI	$30.78	1%

Source: AlphaClone.

FIGURE 35 – 13F PERFORMANCE, 2000–2014

2000-2014	Clone	S&P 500
Return	11.86%	4.31%
Volatility	17.84%	15.24%
Sharpe (1.83%)	0.56	0.16
Drawdown	-47.90%	-50.95%

Year	Clone	S&P 500	Difference
2000	34.4%	-8.2%	42.6%
2001	-4.3%	-11.9%	7.6%
2002	-16.5%	-22.1%	5.6%
2003	11.3%	28.7%	-17.4%
2004	18.0%	10.9%	7.1%
2005	21.0%	4.9%	16.1%
2006	25.8%	15.8%	10.0%
2007	20.2%	5.5%	14.7%
2008	-45.4%	-37.0%	-8.4%
2009	77.5%	26.5%	51.0%
2010	11.3%	15.1%	-3.8%
2011	6.2%	2.1%	4.1%
2012	3.5%	16.0%	-12.5%
2013	51.7%	32.4%	19.3%
2014	15.8%	13.7%	2.1%

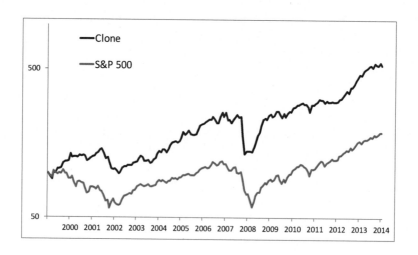

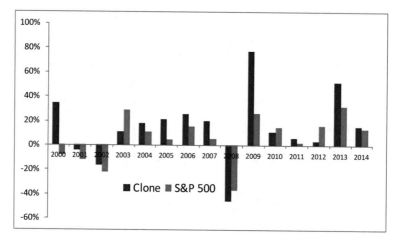

Source: AlphaClone.

CHAPTER 18

RUANNE, CUNIFF & GOLDFARB, SEQUOIA FUND

Followers of modern value investing trace its roots back to a course taught at Columbia University in the 1950s by author and instructor Benjamin Graham. Warren Buffett took it. William Ruane was a classmate.

Buffett went on to a storied career as a value investor, and with a little help from Buffett, so did Ruane. And now Ruane's successors are carrying on his legacy.

Together with another Graham devotee, Richard Cunniff, Ruane formed Ruane, Cunniff & Stires in 1969 and launched its signature vehicle, the Sequoia Fund. Some of the first investors in the fund came through recommendations from Buffett.

The firm changed its name to Ruane, Cunniff & Goldfarb after Richard Goldfarb joined in 1971 right out of Harvard Business School. Buffett's hand was again in evidence. Goldfarb's father had met Buffett and mentioned that his son was looking for an investment job. Buffett suggested getting in touch with Ruane and Cunniff.

Ruane died in 2005, and Cunniff in 2014, leaving Goldfarb at the helm. Judging from the results, the firm and its fund remain in capable hands.

Morningstar named Goldfarb and his Sequoia Fund colleague David Poppe the Domestic-Equity Managers of the Year for 2010. Of significance is that Sequoia earned some of its biggest gains that year in stocks that it held for five or more years—a testament to the firm's long-term investment horizon.

How well does Sequoia perform? According to a 2014 Bloomberg article, Sequoia Fund produced better results than 99 percent of its mutual fund competitors over the past three years and outperformed the S&P 500 by 3 percentage points annually for the previous 25 years. This is despite Sequoia losing money and underperforming the S&P 500 the first four years in business. Talk about perseverance!

Sequoia's results are a testament to the enduring power of value investing paired with concentrated positions and long holding periods. For example, Sequoia ended 2013 with 52 percent of its assets invested in just eight companies, and one of those top companies was Buffett's Berkshire Hathaway. Berkshire has been in the portfolio for more than two decades and at one point represented more than a third of the portfolio. It had dropped down to about 11 percent by 2011. That is about where it stood in early 2014, with the firm managing more than $18 billion.

Cunniff noted in 1976 that his stock picks were out of step with conventional wisdom on Wall Street, particularly when it came to high-flying momentum stocks. "We were orphans when everybody else was rushing after all those so-called one-decision growth stocks. I think that is one of the reasons why our record is so good."

Companies in the firm's portfolio tend to be the type that can be purchased at a discount, have solid management and fundamentals, and are not Wall Street darlings.

The types of companies it owns, how it selects them, and how long it owns its positions prompted one Sequoia investor to quip that the firm runs "the kind of portfolio Buffett might have if he ran a mutual fund."

One change that Goldfarb has brought is a greater emphasis on corporate management. "We're betting more on the jockey and a little less on the horse," he said in 2011.

Unfortunately, the firm has been in the press for another reason lately, and this is a large concentrated stock position that has been tanking.

We have talked in this book about how it can pay to invest alongside stock pickers who are consistent winners. That's true—except when it's not. Even the best players sometimes bet on losers, and sometimes they all seem to do it on the same stock. Here, then is a cautionary tale about crowded trades: stocks that get an unusually high level of hedge fund attention.

Hedge fund darlings can be dangerous. Case in Point: Valeant Pharmaceuticals International (VRX), one of the hottest recent trades among an unusually large number of hedge fund managers, several of whom we profiled in this book. Valeant has been a major contributor to Sequoia's returns and was the largest holding in the portfolio as of the start of 2014. Some other fund managers, like Bill Ackman of Pershing Square and Jeff Ubben of ValueAct, built particularly large and concentrated positions in VRX, which was great when the stock was on the rise but disastrous when it crashed. Anyone who tried to piggyback on Ackman or one of the other managers who built large positions in the stock but got the timing wrong could have suffered mightily.

VRX traded at about $126 in November, 2014 and peaked at $262 in August, 2015, doubling in value. Then VRX got caught up in a controversy over its drug pricing that brought unwanted attention from Congress and federal officials. Other questions about the company's business prospects arose. VRX tanked. By November, 2015, the stock was trading around $70.

A lot of managers got out as the stock fell. As my friend Stan Altshuler, the chief research officer at financial firm Novus, pointed out in an analysis of activity in the stock, hedge funds were mostly selling VRX in the third quarter of 2015 as the price collapsed. But that broad retreat wasn't revealed until they filed with the SEC, which was mid-November, 45 days after the end of the quarter. Altshuler estimated 73 hedge funds sold out their positions in VRX in the quarter and another 19 reduced their positions. VRX continued crashing in October and early November, losing another $100 per share in value.

But not all sold out, and in fact a number increased their positions in the third quarter of 2015, including star traders like Viking Global, Lone Pine, and Maverick. Ackman was still so confident in the company that he announced he had purchased an additional two million shares in October, when the stock had fallen to around $80.

Whether Ackman and the others who added to their positions will eventually profit from the trade—only time will tell. But the moral for investors who try to piggyback on star hedge fund managers was clear: beware of crowded trades in hot companies, particularly when those stocks have already become one of the largest positions in a manager's portfolio.

FIGURE 36 – 13F CURRENT HOLDINGS AS OF SEPTEMBER 30, 2015; PRICE AS OF NOVEMBER 20, 2015

Company	Symbol	Price	% of Portfolio
Allergan plc	AGN	$312.46	31%
Time Warner Cable Inc	TWC	$184.50	9%
Vipshop Holdings	VIPS	$16.35	7%
Align Technology Inc	ALGN	$67.19	5%
Jumei International Holding Class A	JMEI	$ 8.86	5%
LIBERTY GLOBAL PLC	LILAK	$ 0.00	4%
Cable ONE Inc	CABO	$440.64	3%
Kraft Heinz Co	KHC	$73.65	3%
Symetra Financial Corp	SYA	$31.55	3%
Time Warner Inc	TWX	$70.72	3%

Source: AlphaClone.

FIGURE 37 – 13F PERFORMANCE, 2000–2014

2000-2014	Clone	S&P 500
Return	13.65%	4.31%
Volatility	18.51%	15.24%
Sharpe (1.83%)	0.64	0.16
Drawdown	-42.71%	-50.95%

Year	Clone	S&P 500	Difference
2000	28.2%	-8.2%	36.4%
2001	8.2%	-11.9%	20.1%
2002	-8.2%	-22.1%	13.9%
2003	27.7%	28.7%	-1.0%
2004	11.0%	10.9%	0.1%
2005	7.1%	4.9%	2.2%
2006	3.2%	15.8%	-12.6%
2007	5.9%	5.5%	0.4%
2008	-26.4%	-37.0%	10.6%
2009	27.2%	26.5%	0.7%
2010	25.5%	15.1%	10.4%
2011	26.8%	2.1%	24.7%
2012	23.1%	16.0%	7.1%
2013	44.5%	32.4%	12.1%
2014	21.7%	13.7%	8.0%

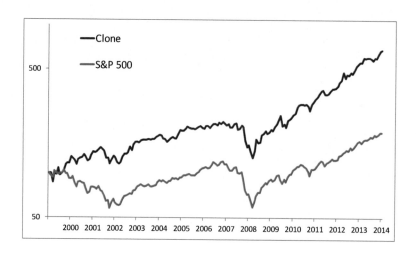

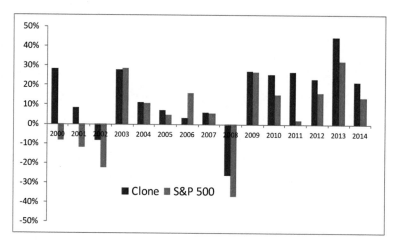

Source: AlphaClone.

CHAPTER 19

SOUTHERNSUN ASSET MANAGEMENT, MICHAEL COOK

Back in 1989, when the old Union Planters Bank of Memphis sold its asset management business, money manager Michael Cook, a Memphis native, found himself without a job. So he made one up, launching SouthernSun Asset Management in his hometown as an investment vehicle through which he could manage client money and practice his brand of value investing with a focus on smaller companies.

As it turned out, losing his job at Planters Bank was a very good thing for Cook's career and for the clients who followed him to his new firm. Today SouthernSun manages more than $5 billion through mutual funds and separately managed accounts for institutional clients.

In 2012, *Bloomberg Markets* magazine named the SouthernSun Small Cap Fund the top fund in the small-cap category, with an annualized average return of 41.1 percent for each of the three years ending in February 2012. The same fund won the 2014 Lipper Award for Best Fund over 5 Years in the Small-Cap Core Funds category.

That's not bad for a guy who started out studying religion and philosophy at Covenant College in Lookout Mountain, Georgia, and whose bio on the firm's website lists no university degrees. That bio does include one other education reference: attendance at the OCCA Business Programme, Wycliffe Hall, University of Oxford. Cook started out in finance as a broker in the Memphis office of Merrill Lynch & Co. before moving to the trust department of Union Planters Bank.

At SouthernSun, Cook relies on extensive fundamental research to drive his stock selection. He has traditionally focused on small to mid-sized companies and looks for businesses with a niche or edge, strong management and a sound balance sheet with good cash flow. "We pour over the financials, visit the management," he says. "I have to be able to understand who the critical decision makers are."

What Cook doesn't do is pay much attention to the algorithms and quantitative methods that some other investors use to guide their trades. "We very rarely use quantitative screens," Cook says. "We do our own work. We visit companies, we visit management, we visit their facilities, we visit their suppliers. We go to industry trade shows more frequently than sell-side, Wall Street investor conferences."

Among his bankable plays that were cited by Bloomberg in its award were two companies that returned an annualized 75 percent for the three years ending March 12, 2012: Darling International Inc. and Tractor Supply Co.

His two main US funds today, the SouthernSun Small Cap Fund and the SouthernSun US Equity Fund, have total assets around $1.3 billion. Both run concentrated books of twenty to forty positions and limit any single holding to a maximum of 10 percent of the portfolio. The US Equity Fund invests in companies with market capitalizations of $1-$12 billion. The Small Cap Fund looks for companies in the $500 million to $3.5 billion range.

In 2006, Phillip Cook, son of the founder, joined the firm and serves as a partner and senior analyst. Although there are now two Cooks in the firm, it is no longer a family business after its sale in 2013. The buyer, Affiliated Managers Group, is a global asset management company that runs a larger family of mutual funds and other investment vehicles, with total assets under management of more than $600 billion. Both Cooks remain on board with long-term commitments to continue using the patient, value investment methods that worked well for the firm in the past.

FIGURE 38 – 13F CURRENT HOLDINGS AS OF SEPTEMBER 30, 2015; PRICE AS OF NOVEMBER 20, 2015

Company	Symbol	Price	% of Portfolio
Darling Ingredients Inc	DAR	$ 9.39	6%
AGCO Corp	AGCO	$48.64	6%
Chicago Bridge & Iron Company NV	CBI	$41.92	5%
Centene Corp	CNC	$57.42	5%
Clean Harbors Inc	CLH	$41.59	5%
OGE Energy Corp	OGE	$26.06	4%
Broadridge Financial Solutions Inc	BR	$55.85	4%
Trinity Industries Inc	TRN	$26.29	4%
Newfield Exploration Co	NFX	$37.78	4%
IDEX Corp	IEX	$78.34	4%

Source: AlphaClone.

FIGURE 39 – 13F PERFORMANCE, 2000–2014

2000-2014	Clone	S&P 500
Return	14.49%	4.31%
Volatility	25.41%	15.24%
Sharpe (1.83%)	0.50	0.16
Drawdown	-62.95%	-50.95%

Year	Clone	S&P 500	Difference
2000	22.3%	-8.2%	30.5%
2001	-2.4%	-11.9%	9.5%
2002	-10.1%	-22.1%	12.0%
2003	47.1%	28.7%	18.4%
2004	30.4%	10.9%	19.5%
2005	13.2%	4.9%	8.3%
2006	16.3%	15.8%	0.5%
2007	21.4%	5.5%	15.9%
2008	-39.9%	-37.0%	-2.9%
2009	32.8%	26.5%	6.3%
2010	49.3%	15.1%	34.2%
2011	18.5%	2.1%	16.4%
2012	17.4%	16.0%	1.4%
2013	42.2%	32.4%	9.8%
2014	-1.6%	13.7%	-15.3%

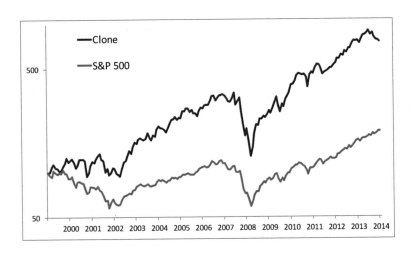

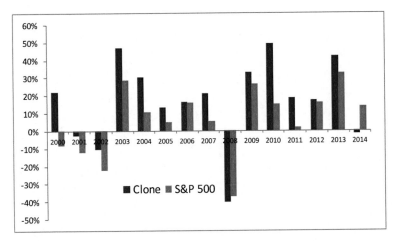

Source: AlphaClone.

CHAPTER 20

SPO ADVISORY CORP., JOHN SCULLY

Back a few decades ago, if you were serious about studying economics and finance, one of the places to get plugged into the latest thinking was the Stanford Graduate School of Business, which boasted two economics Nobel laureates on its faculty, Myron Scholes and William Sharpe. But there was another professor not nearly as well known who taught a finance class in which he preached the principles of value investing. Prof. John McDonald influenced several future fund management superstars.

Two of those students were John Scully (no relation to the former Apple CEO) and William Oberndorf. After graduating and working with Texas investor Robert Bass for several years, Scully and Oberndorf teamed up with a more recent Stanford Business School graduate, William Patterson, to form SPO Partners in Mill Valley, Ca. in 1989. SPO has since grown into a $10 billion fund that quietly churns out enviable returns through a combination of value investing techniques and a concentrated portfolio.

Scully is now the only one of the three still at the firm. Patterson died in 2010 at 48 and Oberndorf retired in 2012 to start a private investment vehicle, Oberndorf Enterprises. But the dedication to the founding principles remains, with investments concentrated in a few high-conviction, carefully selected companies and a strategy that moves between long equity investment and private equity.

Scully explained the investment philosophy as part of a speech he delivered at Stanford in 2002: "What we are attempting to do is to bring capital to managements that merit it in businesses that have outstanding characteristics."

One of the more celebrated deals orchestrated by SPO was its investment in Plum Creek Timber in the 1990s. SPO bought control of Plum Creek, which owned vast expanses of timber in the West. The move to protect the spotted owl prompted the government to close federal lands to logging, which sent the value of timberland in private hands soaring. Plum Creek became the largest private timber owner in the United States, and the value of the investment increased tenfold.

SPO has found the value it sought in a wide variety of businesses and industries, from high-tech to hotels and from a German cable company to a US producer of concrete. What it does not do is focus its investments on very many companies at the same time, running a portfolio with only a dozen or so companies and with the biggest chunk of money placed with the top five or six. SPO holds onto favorite positions for years. As of the first quarter of 2014, SPO had fourteen positions.

SPO often takes large enough positions to merit corporate board seats. Scully was a board member of Plum Creek. Patterson was chairman of another SPO investment, the power company Calpine.

The death of Patterson and the departure of Oberndorf left Scully to manage SPO, which he now does with two younger SPO managing directors, Edward McDermott and Eli Weinberg. The two newcomers have a familiar pedigree, both holding MBAs from Stanford Business School.

FIGURE 40 – 13F CURRENT HOLDINGS AS OF SEPTEMBER 30, 2015; PRICE AS OF NOVEMBER 20, 2015

Company	Symbol	Price	% of Portfolio
Equinix	EQIX	$298.60	16%
Charter Communications Inc Class /	CHTR	$186.48	16%
Pioneer Natural Resources Co	PXD	$141.21	15%
Liberty Global PLC Class C	LBTYK	$40.86	11%
Charles Schwab Corp	SCHW	$33.34	10%
Qualcomm Inc	QCOM	$49.62	9%
LPL Financial Holdings Inc	LPLA	$44.58	6%
Monsanto Co	MON	$96.09	5%
Oasis Petroleum Inc	OAS	$11.36	3%
Range Resources Corp	RRC	$30.41	3%

Source: AlphaClone.

FIGURE 41 – 13F PERFORMANCE, 2000–2014

2000-2014	Clone	S&P 500
Return	14.71%	4.31%
Volatility	18.58%	15.24%
Sharpe (1.83%)	0.69	0.16
Drawdown	-60.65%	-50.95%

Year	Clone	S&P 500	Difference
2000	21.4%	-8.2%	29.6%
2001	6.1%	-11.9%	18.0%
2002	-2.1%	-22.1%	20.0%
2003	116.7%	28.7%	88.0%
2004	27.0%	10.9%	16.1%
2005	9.7%	4.9%	4.8%
2006	14.1%	15.8%	-1.7%
2007	2.7%	5.5%	-2.8%
2008	-57.1%	-37.0%	-20.1%
2009	62.4%	26.5%	35.9%
2010	30.9%	15.1%	15.8%
2011	-2.7%	2.1%	-4.8%
2012	33.6%	16.0%	17.6%
2013	43.1%	32.4%	10.7%
2014	14.6%	13.7%	0.9%

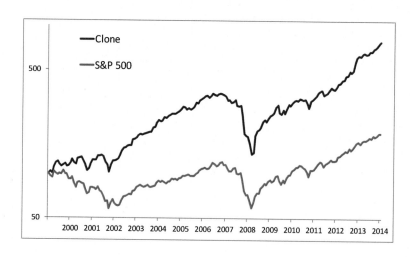

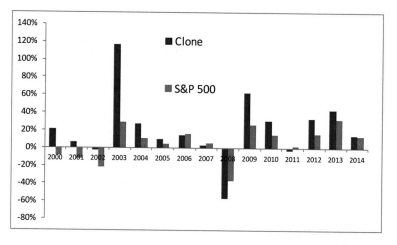

Source: AlphaClone.

CHAPTER 21

THIRD POINT MANAGEMENT, DAN LOEB

When it comes to corporate management, Daniel Loeb is rarely at a loss for words, and they are frequently not very nice words. As founder and CEO of Third Point, an event-driven value hedge fund based in New York, Loeb manages $14 billion in assets, which he uses to make strategic investments in companies he thinks have lost their way. He uses his position to push for change that he can capitalize upon, and he is not very subtle in how he goes about playing at shareholder activism.

His letters to companies in which he invests are legendary. New Yorker magazine dubbed him "Wall Street's merchant of venom."

Loeb once wrote to Intercept Inc., calling for the CEO to resign and branding its senior management "among the worst that we have witnessed in our investment career."

He penned a letter to Ligand Pharmaceuticals, castigating its management and calling for the ousting of its CEO, David Robinson, and its CFO, Paul Maier.[14] "I must wonder how in this day and age the Company's Board of Directors has not held you and

Paul Maier responsible for your respective failures and shown you both the door long ago—accompanied by a well-worn boot planted in the backside."

Sometimes he gets downright personal. He once took aim at the grandsons of the founder of a paper company, calling them members of the "Lucky Sperm Club."

Loeb's letters to corporations are must-reads on Wall Street, and not just for their creative spite. Followers of Third Point know that when Loeb is in attack mode, corporate change is likely to follow, which typically results in profit for Loeb and those who invest alongside him.

In 2013, for example, Third Point realized a 25-percent gain on its investments thanks to some well-placed bets. Loeb helped orchestrate a management change at Yahoo that led to a jump in the stock price; he promptly cashed out. He went head-to-head against fellow activist investor William Ackman of Pershing Square. Ackman had taken a major short position in Herbalife and loudly proclaimed the company a mess. Loeb took the other side of the bet and booked a quick profit in 2013 when the stock price rose.

For someone who seems so focused on a few select companies, Loeb runs a rather diversified portfolio. He has also been actively involved in buying and selling debt, including mortgage-backed securities.

Loeb in fact has considerable background in debt investment. Before launching Third Point in 1995, he was vice president of high-yield bond sales at Citigroup, and before that he worked in the distressed debt department of Jeffries & Co.

Loeb grew up in Southern California and maintains the trappings of the California lifestyle. He is a lifelong surfer and a devotee of Ashtanga yoga. After obtaining a bachelor's degree in economics from Columbia University, he started his career as a private equity associate at Warburg Pincus.

His Third Point investments have made him a billionaire and

landed him in ninth place on the *Institutional Investors' Alpha* magazine 2014 Rich List, with an estimated $700 million in earnings for 2013.

As for mellowing with age: not much chance. One of his more recent targets was Dow Chemical Co., which he noted has "a poor operational track record across multiple business segments."

But he can sometimes be persuaded to change his tune. After becoming the biggest shareholder in auction house Sotheby's, Loeb spent months lambasting CEO William Ruprecht. By the time Loeb finally gained a seat on the board, Ruprecht had instituted significant changes. Loeb did an about face and joined other board members in offering support for Ruprecht and his team. (For more information and analysis of Third Point, view this Novus analysis of the fund.[15])

FIGURE 42 – 13F CURRENT HOLDINGS AS OF SEPTEMBER 30, 2015; PRICE AS OF NOVEMBER 20, 2015

Company	Symbol	Price	% of Portfolio
Baxter International Inc	BAX	$38.31	17%
Amgen Inc	AMGN	$159.91	13%
Allergan plc	AGN	$312.46	10%
Dow Chemical Co	DOW	$53.32	10%
Yum! Brands Inc	YUM	$72.76	9%
Kraft Heinz Co	KHC	$73.65	6%
Mohawk Industries Inc	MHK	$192.29	4%
T-Mobile US Inc	TMUS	$38.44	3%
Roper Technologies Inc	ROP	$191.49	2%
Sealed Air Corp	SEE	$45.33	2%

Source: AlphaClone.

FIGURE 43 – 13F PERFORMANCE, 2000–2014

2000-2014	Clone	S&P 500
Return	12.89%	4.31%
Volatility	19.83%	15.24%
Sharpe (1.83%)	0.56	0.16
Drawdown	-56.48%	-50.95%

Year	Clone	S&P 500	Difference
2000	-17.0%	-8.2%	-8.8%
2001	4.9%	-11.9%	16.8%
2002	-8.3%	-22.1%	13.8%
2003	59.4%	28.7%	30.7%
2004	55.8%	10.9%	44.9%
2005	46.3%	4.9%	41.4%
2006	11.7%	15.8%	-4.1%
2007	7.2%	5.5%	1.7%
2008	-42.2%	-37.0%	-5.2%
2009	15.9%	26.5%	-10.6%
2010	25.8%	15.1%	10.7%
2011	-0.2%	2.1%	-2.3%
2012	30.9%	16.0%	14.9%
2013	41.4%	32.4%	9.0%
2014	13.9%	13.7%	0.2%

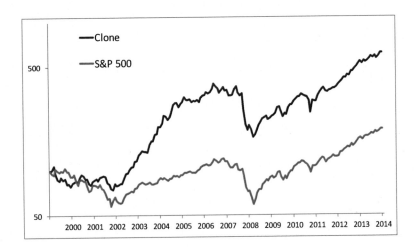

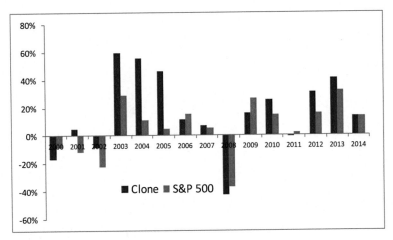

Source: AlphaClone.

CHAPTER 22

YACKTMAN ASSET MANAGEMENT, DONALD YACKTMAN

When he's researching a company for possible investment, value investor Donald Yacktman reads everything he can get his hands— or his computer terminal—on. What he doesn't do is talk to the company's management.

Unlike some stock pickers who depend on direct contact with a company and its management to fill in the blanks before deciding on an investment, Yacktman prefers to do his research at arm's length. "The danger of talking to managers is that they tell you what you want to hear, not necessarily what you want to know," he once said.

Yacktman's approach has been effective enough to give him and his Yacktman Asset Management, based in Austin, Texas, a track record worthy of notice. Morningstar named him Portfolio Manager of the Year for his performance in 1991, nominated him for Fund Manager of the Decade in 2009, and named him a finalist for Domestic-Stock Manager of the Year in 2011. Mutual Fund Letter named him Portfolio Manager of the Year for 1994.

Not bad for someone who trolls for opportunity among

often-unglamorous companies that he believes have long-term possibilities but may not be particularly popular plays at the moment he makes them. At one point in the late 1990s, he put his money on non-tech small-cap stocks, missing the tech boom of the late 1990s. Some of his own board members were so upset by his lagging returns that they tried unsuccessfully to fire him. He was, of course, ultimately proven right when the tech bubble burst and his own portfolio shot up, beating the market for three straight years.

Yacktman preaches patience and likes long holding periods for his picks. As he noted in a discussion of his methods, "We're not usually looking for the scruffy cyclical or turnaround story, but for businesses with high market shares in their principle product or service lines, with long product cycles but short customer-re-purchase cycles, and with relatively low capital requirements that allow the company to generate high cash returns on tangible assets while growing."

Where that leads is to companies like PepsiCo and Procter & Gamble, which were among his biggest plays in 2011. He was a major investor in Rupert Murdoch's News Corp., realizing strong gains in 2011 and holding onto his position through the steep subsequent decline in the company's stock.

Yacktman founded his mutual fund company in 1992 after serving as a portfolio manager for Selected American Shares mutual fund. Before that he was a portfolio manager and partner at Stein Roe & Farnham. He graduated magna cum laude with a BS in economics from the University of Utah and earned an MBA with distinction from Harvard University.

While Yacktman's picks don't always look pretty at the start, they tend to pan out given enough time. Case in point: Amer-iCredit. Yacktman owned it for four years when it took a dive, falling from a high of around $27 in June 2007 to about $7 in July 2008. Yacktman decided to double down, buying more at $7 and still more when the stock went to $3.60. It took a little less than two years for the company's stock to rebound, rising to around $20 and giving Yacktman gains on his bargain buys ranging from 200 percent to more than 500 percent.

FIGURE 44 – 13F CURRENT HOLDINGS AS OF SEPTEMBER 30, 2015; PRICE AS OF NOVEMBER 20, 2015

Company	Symbol	Price	% of Portfolio
Procter & Gamble Co	PG	$75.82	13%
PepsiCo Inc	PEP	$100.10	11%
Twenty-First Century Fox Inc Class /	FOXA	$30.07	7%
Sysco Corp	SYY	$40.92	7%
Coca-Cola Co	KO	$42.43	7%
Oracle Corp	ORCL	$39.34	6%
Cisco Systems Inc	CSCO	$27.57	6%
Twenty-First Century Fox Inc Class I	FOX	$30.54	6%
Microsoft Corp	MSFT	$54.19	5%
Johnson & Johnson	JNJ	$102.48	5%

Source: AlphaClone.

FIGURE 45 – 13F PERFORMANCE, 2000–2014

2000-2014	Clone	S&P 500
Return	13.79%	4.31%
Volatility	16.64%	15.24%
Sharpe (1.83%)	0.72	0.16
Drawdown	-44.87%	-50.95%

Year	Clone	S&P 500	Difference
2000	25.3%	-8.2%	33.5%
2001	18.4%	-11.9%	30.3%
2002	3.4%	-22.1%	25.5%
2003	23.3%	28.7%	-5.4%
2004	13.0%	10.9%	2.1%
2005	-7.0%	4.9%	-11.9%
2006	16.7%	15.8%	0.9%
2007	-0.9%	5.5%	-6.4%
2008	-25.5%	-37.0%	11.5%
2009	77.1%	26.5%	50.6%
2010	15.3%	15.1%	0.2%
2011	12.3%	2.1%	10.2%
2012	13.3%	16.0%	-2.7%
2013	32.8%	32.4%	0.4%
2014	17.7%	13.7%	4.0%

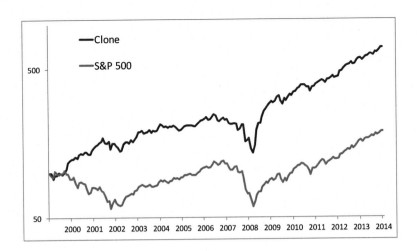

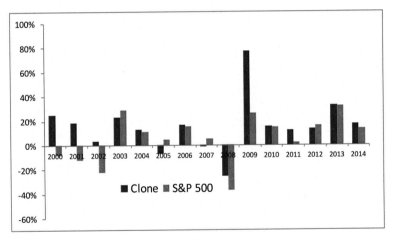

Source: AlphaClone.

CHAPTER 23

FUND GROUPS AND STRATEGIES

Instead of just tracking one manager, who may be going through that nasty divorce or growing complacent in his wealth, an investor can create a hedge fund of funds by combining a number of funds into one portfolio. The investor could simply take the top ten holdings from each fund and update the portfolio in the same method as before. This option gives the investor the additional benefit of diversifying his or her risk across multiple managers.

First, we will look at the performance of the twenty funds individually.

FIGURE 46 – 13F PERFORMANCE, 2000–2014

Year	S&P 500	Berkshire Clone	Appaloosa Clone	Ariel Clone	Avenir Clone	Barrow Hanley Clone	Baupost Clone	Brave Warrior Clone	Cobalt Clone	Eminence Clone	Eagle Clone
2000	-8.2%	22.8%	38.2%	59.4%	13.3%	33.4%	9.6%	13.7%	-1.2%	23.8%	58.5%
2001	-11.9%	5.4%	28.8%	14.5%	-4.7%	-6.1%	38.1%	4.6%	-6.7%	5.7%	0.8%
2002	-22.1%	-0.9%	-16.8%	2.2%	-11.4%	-3.2%	-11.2%	-0.7%	-17.6%	-18.3%	-2.3%
2003	28.7%	26.8%	74.6%	34.6%	92.7%	33.8%	95.1%	42.9%	52.8%	50.6%	31.4%
2004	10.9%	10.9%	46.7%	20.9%	38.9%	20.2%	19.3%	31.3%	49.8%	29.9%	15.8%
2005	4.9%	7.3%	148.0%	10.6%	12.0%	19.3%	-10.7%	18.0%	43.6%	8.7%	5.2%
2006	15.8%	21.7%	32.0%	14.8%	18.2%	18.3%	21.9%	20.9%	5.8%	19.6%	13.3%
2007	5.5%	-2.1%	2.8%	12.7%	1.1%	11.1%	-15.7%	1.6%	27.9%	7.1%	6.5%
2008	-37.0%	-19.0%	-48.0%	-47.4%	-54.2%	-27.6%	-47.1%	-46.5%	-57.7%	-26.7%	-28.5%
2009	26.5%	21.0%	123.2%	95.6%	67.0%	16.4%	62.1%	39.6%	68.9%	23.5%	14.1%
2010	15.1%	13.9%	23.0%	23.4%	36.2%	4.6%	54.7%	21.2%	10.9%	21.3%	24.0%
2011	2.1%	11.5%	-28.8%	-11.5%	12.5%	4.3%	3.9%	9.2%	-12.6%	-1.0%	7.1%
2012	16.0%	12.4%	45.3%	26.0%	23.3%	9.2%	-7.2%	19.1%	31.4%	22.1%	22.0%
2013	32.4%	25.8%	52.4%	42.9%	30.2%	33.6%	43.5%	60.6%	33.9%	40.2%	36.3%
2014	13.7%	10.8%	14.4%	15.3%	18.1%	11.1%	29.4%	24.7%	16.1%	7.7%	11.1%

Year	S&P 500	Raiff Clone	Gardner Russo Clone	Greenlight Clone	LSV Clone	Par Clone	Ruanne Cardiff Clone	Southern Sun Clone	SPO Clone	Third Point Clone	Yackltman Clone
2000	-8.2%	34.4%	38.6%	48.6%	10.9%	11.0%	28.2%	22.3%	21.4%	-17.0%	25.3%
2001	-11.9%	-4.3%	2.7%	18.7%	-6.5%	-17.4%	8.2%	-2.4%	6.1%	4.9%	18.4%
2002	-22.1%	-16.5%	-1.1%	-20.0%	-11.0%	-12.3%	-8.2%	-10.1%	-2.1%	-8.3%	3.4%
2003	28.7%	11.3%	23.8%	75.6%	37.0%	65.6%	27.7%	47.1%	116.7%	59.4%	23.3%
2004	10.9%	18.0%	6.4%	44.6%	26.4%	10.4%	11.0%	30.4%	27.0%	55.8%	13.0%
2005	4.9%	21.0%	1.9%	21.7%	18.4%	15.9%	7.1%	13.2%	9.7%	46.3%	-7.0%
2006	15.8%	25.8%	24.7%	17.9%	32.5%	40.8%	3.2%	16.3%	14.1%	11.7%	16.7%
2007	5.5%	20.2%	7.7%	-13.0%	6.8%	8.1%	5.9%	21.4%	2.7%	7.2%	-0.9%
2008	-37.0%	-45.4%	-29.3%	-39.1%	-25.2%	-38.3%	-26.4%	-39.9%	-57.1%	-42.2%	-25.5%
2009	26.5%	77.5%	25.3%	27.2%	5.2%	70.1%	27.2%	32.8%	62.4%	15.9%	77.1%
2010	15.1%	11.3%	20.7%	17.7%	10.8%	14.4%	25.5%	49.3%	30.9%	25.8%	15.3%
2011	2.1%	6.2%	4.0%	-6.9%	-1.5%	-2.5%	26.8%	18.5%	-2.7%	-0.2%	12.3%
2012	16.0%	3.5%	27.1%	11.4%	15.8%	29.6%	23.1%	17.4%	33.6%	30.9%	13.3%
2013	32.4%	51.7%	24.4%	35.6%	29.4%	75.4%	44.5%	42.2%	43.1%	41.4%	32.8%
2014	13.7%	15.8%	6.7%	10.9%	13.2%	24.2%	21.7%	-1.6%	14.6%	13.9%	17.7%

Below, we look at taking the top ten stocks from each manager profiled in this book for a 200 stock portfolio (including Buffett). The size of this portfolio may be unrealistic for some, but not for the institutional readers. This hybrid FOF experienced 10 percentage points of outperformance with stock-like volatility and a similar drawdown of the broad index. To try and be intellectually honest, we also include the small-cap index to demonstrate that some of the alpha was likely just investing in anything other than the large-cap index at bubble valuations in 2000. A more robust method would be to combine a number of managers whose methodologies differ substantially, and the volatility and drawdown could decrease further.

FIGURE 47 – 13F PERFORMANCE, 2000–2014

2000-2014	Clone	S&P 500	Small Cap
Return	14.18%	4.31%	9.00%
Volatility	16.03%	15.24%	19.09%
Sharpe (1.83%)	0.77	0.16	0.38
Drawdown	-51.99%	-50.95%	-50.57%

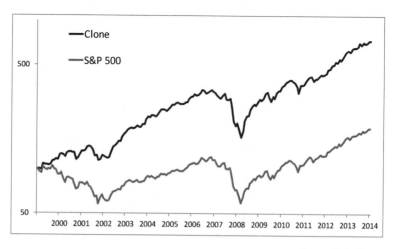

Source: AlphaClone.

Many ask if tracking the top 1, 3, or 5 stock portfolios instead of 10 stock portfolios would be more ideal. Or, would weighting the portfolio like the manager does instead of equal-weighting be better? Below is a table that summarizes the various weightings. For the most part, holding anywhere from three to ten stocks is best. And equal weighting seems to be better than manager weighting, but broadly similar. For most of the managers we include in the book and the Appendix the worst idea is to track or include the top holding. It is by far the worst performer! (Top 10 M is the manager weighted portfolio.)

FIGURE 48 – 13F PERFORMANCE, VARIOUS WEIGHTINGS, 2000–2014

	Average of All Managers
Top 1	8.78%
Top 3	12.40%
Top 5	13.15%
Top 10	13.34%
Top 10 M	12.78%

Source: AlphaClone

	Berkshire Clone	Appaloosa Clone	Ariel Clone	Avenir Clone	Barrow Hanley Clone	Baupost Clone	Brave Warrior Clone	Cobalt Clone	Eminence Clone	Eagle Clone
Top 1	2.47%	2.04%	20.19%	3.73%	10.42%	2.80%	0.96%	19.53%	10.87%	3.65%
Top 3	6.88%	9.27%	16.25%	9.81%	10.42%	4.37%	9.81%	14.29%	12.22%	17.99%
Top 5	7.87%	21.26%	16.42%	12.27%	10.42%	14.25%	11.82%	16.94%	11.66%	15.94%
Top 10	10.53%	20.94%	16.38%	14.49%	10.63%	13.66%	13.88%	10.99%	12.18%	12.74%
Top 10 M	7.04%	15.82%	16.64%	13.21%	10.74%	13.56%	11.50%	10.99%	12.48%	15.31%

	Raiff Clone	Gardner Russo Clone	Greenlight Clone	LSV Clone	Par Clone	Ruanne Cardiff Clone	Southern Sun Clone	SPO Clone	Third Point Clone	Yackltman Clone
Top 1	15.52%	3.76%	12.06%	10.55%	6.26%	12.97%	4.17%	14.74%	6.48%	12.38%
Top 3	10.92%	11.30%	14.31%	7.70%	21.84%	13.46%	9.79%	16.94%	13.19%	17.30%
Top 5	9.76%	10.23%	10.61%	5.60%	14.05%	15.66%	15.38%	18.20%	10.59%	14.14%
Top 10	11.86%	10.96%	13.12%	9.51%	15.38%	13.65%	14.49%	14.71%	12.89%	13.79%
Top 10 M	9.94%	10.44%	12.63%	8.51%	14.96%	13.94%	14.40%	15.62%	13.14%	14.76%

Another application of fund groups is applying a consensus approach to a portfolio. This tactic involves purchasing the stocks that are held by more than one fund manager. The thesis here is that a stock selection is validated when more than one prominent investor has come to the same conclusion on a security. One good group here to track would be the "Tiger Cubs."

If you had to name the top hedge fund managers ever, Julian H. Robertson would certainly be on the list. Robertson successfully ran funds under the Tiger name for many years, and an entire book about Robertson has been written, entitled *Julian Robertson: A Tiger in the Land of Bulls and Bears*. The Tiger funds reached a peak of $22 billion in assets in 1998. After many years of strong out-performance, Robertson suffered large losses, and while the S&P 500 index climbed 21 percent in 1999, the Tiger funds declined 19 percent. Robertson closed his investment company in March 2000 and liquidated its remaining $6 billion in investments.

Although it shut down portfolio management, Tiger is still in operation, albeit in a form resembling an incubator structure for young managers. A manager who has worked at Tiger has essentially earned the hedge fund gold seal of approval. Below, we examine what are likely four of the most famous Cubs (Blue Ridge, Lone Pine, Maverick, and Viking) before trying out some variant strategies.

Blue Ridge Capital

In the broad Tiger line of hedge fund managers who claim some connection to legendary Tiger Management founder Julian Robertson, probably none can boast a link closer than John Griffin's. Before he founded his own hedge fund, Blue Ridge Capital, Griffin served as president of Tiger Management under Robertson. Griffin is regarded as perhaps Robertson's closest advisor and has been credited with helping scout for recruits to Tiger, many of whom now run their own hedge funds.

Tiger alumni are notoriously publicity-shy, but Griffin may be the shyest of the bunch, almost never offering a comment that is picked up and published. At a rare public speech in 2013 at the University of Virginia, his alma mater, Griffin offered up some comments about his mentor and how Robertson was able to collect such a formidable stable of talent at Tiger Global: "Julian was always willing to take a risk by hiring young people who were smart, competitive, and honest."

After graduating from the University of Virginia, Griffin landed a job in the Morgan Stanley merchant banking division, leaving in 1987 to join Tiger. Robertson promoted him to president in 1993, a post he held for three years before leaving to launch Blue Ridge in 1996.

At Blue Ridge, Griffin employs the same long-short equity strategy that was Tiger's forte and is the preferred strategy for so-called Tiger Cubs like him who spun out of Robertson's firm. Griffin takes a bottom-up approach to research, looking at everything from a company's balance sheet to its earnings growth and valuation. It has been said that when it is all boiled down to an investment thesis, he likes it to be clear and simple enough to explain to a 10-year-old.

Griffin has served as an adjunct professor at Columbia University in New York and the University of Virginia in Charlottesville, where students get to partake of his investment wisdom for the price of enrollment. I was a student in 2000, where we used to download and print out 13F filings before each class. We would scrutinize the holdings of the guest speakers and this exercise was the inspiration for the 13F work I started by hand years later.

Blue Ridge's success has made Griffin a rich man, landing him repeatedly on the Institutional Investor's Alpha Rich List for highest paid hedge fund managers.[16] In 2014, he pulled in $470 million, according to Alpha. He did even better in 2008, earning $625 million.

Those big earnings came from savvy stock picks. While many of his most profitable bets in recent years have been in tech and biotech, his past picks have covered a broad range and have included everything from McDonald's to Walgreen Co. He has not always come out on top, but like other Tiger Cubs, he has been in the black with enough consistency to make Blue Ridge a $9 billion behemoth and one of the largest long-short hedge funds around.

Lone Pine Capital

The Tiger name stands tall in the annals of hedge fund superstars, with a long roster of managers who trace their lineage to Julian Robertson. Among those is Stephen Mandel, a former Tiger Management analyst who launched his Lone Pine Capital in 1998 and grew it into one of the largest and most successful of the "Tiger Cubs" that spun out from Tiger Management. Today, Lone Pine manages about $24 billion in assets, and Mandel has become a billionaire, landing on lists of the richest hedge fund managers.

A publicity-shy manager, Mandel has rarely been quoted or interviewed, neither when his stock picks are yielding outsized returns nor when he is lagging. Mandel has had his share of both results, but with the scales decidedly tipped toward the positive. From its launch on January 1, 1998, to mid-July 2015, his flagship Lone Cypress long-short equity fund posted a 16.9-percent annualized return, compared to 6.4 percent for the S&P 500.

Mandel accomplished that feat with old-fashioned, bottom-up analysis and research. His focus from the start has been on companies that can increase value through organic earnings growth and/or are making positive management or strategic moves that have not yet been reflected in valuations. He is drawn to what he calls "blue sky" stories—companies with grand plans and opportunities but that have high valuations and few if any earnings (companies like Tesla and Zillow, two of his recent picks).

In an investor letter jointly signed by Mandel and three of his Lone Pine colleagues, Mandel explained the reasoning behind many of Lone Pine's forays into the world of innovation across a wide range of industries, particularly on Internet-based companies:

"We remain committed to Internet-enabled and enabling businesses globally, companies that are reshaping advertising, entertainment, networking, retailing, and travel, among other industries. We are also invested behind innovation in energy, enterprise software, networks, genomics, manufacturing, and pharmaceuticals." [17]

While Mandel's dedication to deep fundamental research may be informed by value investing principles, his does not conform to that style. He often trades more frequently than most value investors and also plays in expensive tech and biotech stocks that value investors shy away from.

For example, back in 2006, he held three million Apple shares valued at $85 per share. He sold 1.5 million when the stock reached $120 per share and another 250,000 when it hit $150. When it reached $200, he shrank his holding to 600,000 shares. Then Apple hit a speed bump, and the shares dropped to $140. Mandel bought back 2.3 million shares in March 2008, but then sold them by June. He continued to trade in and out of Apple for the next two years.

Part of what hurt Lone Pine's returns in recent years was the lack of shorting opportunities as a raging bull market left few stocks behind. Lone Pine's short positions suffered as a result and dragged down performance. Mandel lamented the problem in letters to investors in 2014. But he predicted that a correction was in order and that Lone Pine was ready to take advantage of it in its short book. "We are poised to take advantage of those companies treading water without swimsuits when the tide eventually goes out," he and his team wrote in a 2014 letter to investors.[18]

Mandel has never forgotten the mentoring provided by Robertson. In one of his rare comments to the press, he offered some observations as part of a 2008 article about Robertson:

"Julian, above all else, impressed upon me the importance of understanding people—the abilities, track records, ethics and character of management, particularly the CEO—not only forming our own impressions but checking out management through our network and former colleagues and others in the same industry." [19]

Maverick Capital

In the select club of Tiger Management alumni who formed their own funds as so-called Tiger Cubs, Lee Ainslie III stands out. He was one of the early recruits to Julian Robertson's Tiger Management, one of the first to strike out on his own, and one of the youngest to leave the nest.

Ainslie was a student at the University of North Carolina when he met Robertson, who was visiting the school. That meeting led to an offer to join the firm, which Ainslie did after graduation in 1990. He only stayed three years, leaving in 1993 at age 28 when he had an opportunity to start Maverick with seed capital from a significant investor. (Note: Ainslie finished his undergrad degree at the Engineering school at Virginia, where all students have to write a thesis. I am probably the only person on the planet that has read his thesis besides his advisor. Likewise, you should be able to find my paper on gene therapy buried deep in the stacks somewhere...)

Today Maverick is a major long-short hedge fund that manages $9 billion, and Ainslie is regarded as an elite stock picker. He was one of the featured characters in the 2007 book *Hedge Hunters: Hedge Fund Masters on the Rewards the Risk and the Reckoning.*

Ainslie's investment process looks at both a company's valuation and its management team, and he has come to pay increasing attention to the quality and strength of management. As he said in an interview, "We have made the mistake more than once of not investing in a company with a great management team because of valuation concerns, only to look back a year later and realize we missed an opportunity because the management team made intelligent, strategic decisions that had a significant impact." [20]

Ainslie started strong with Maverick and generated 17-percent average annual returns between 1995 and 2007, handily beating the S&P 500. But Maverick has stumbled twice since then, first in the market meltdown of 2008, and then again in 2011, when his funds lost anywhere from 15 to 31 percent. He has bounced back since then, but his assets under management, which stood at $11.5 billion at the end of 2007, have stayed around $9 billion.

Maverick uses a number of different valuation methods when researching a company but relies most heavily on comparisons of free cash flow to enterprise value. Ainslie tries to recognize the unique characteristics of different business segments in his valuations, saying, "I believe it is a mistake to evaluate a technology company, a financial company, and a retailer all with the same valuation metric." He likes to hold positions for one to three years.

Maverick uses a bottom-up approach to stock picking and aims its long bets at companies that it estimates will outperform the market by 20 percent on an annualized basis. While he believes that patience is a necessary virtue in portfolio management, he is not averse to changing course on a stock pick if there are clear signals that it is not working out. What he tries to avoid is paying too much attention to broader market swings. As he once said, "The odds of my adding value consistently by trying to time the market are very slim. At the time of maximum pain, you need to maintain your discipline."

Viking Global Investors

When O. Andreas Halvorsen left Tiger Management to form his own hedge fund in 1999, the name he picked for his new company was hardly surprising: Viking Global Investors. Halvorsen is a former Norwegian Navy Special Forces veteran, where he served as a platoon commander, one of the few facts about his early background that he has ever divulged.

As another secretive hedge fund manager, Halvorsen has quietly built Viking into a consistent top performer as a stock picker. Viking now manages more than $31 billion while Halvorsen has amassed a personal fortune estimated at more than $2.8 billion in 2015, which Forbes magazine said made him the eighth richest hedge fund manager and the fourth richest Norwegian.[21]

He has done it using patient, bottom-up stock selection methods based on deep fundamental research that he learned and honed while at Tiger. As another of the early Tiger alumni to strike out on their own, Halvorsen ranks as one of the most successful of the Tiger cubs. His closely watched Viking Global Equities fund produced a 17.7% annualized return from inception in the fourth quarter of 1999 to the end of 2013.

In a rare interview, at the Milken Institute in Santa Monica, Ca. in 2013, he discussed some of his ideas.[22] He said he searches sectors and industries looking for opportunities and focuses a good deal of attention on company management. He talks directly to company management, as well as to competitors, suppliers and others who might help inform an investment decision. Good management teams, he said, are underappreciated for their ability to create value, just as poor managers are often overlooked in their ability to destroy value.

Shorting stocks is a challenge, Halvorsen said, noting, "It's a heart wrenching activity, because you can lose a lot of money doing it." While he has made money on shorts, he has also lost enough to drag down overall results, particularly in recent bull markets. His losing short bets against information technology stocks were a drag on performance in 2013.

Halvorsen tends to favor oversized bets on highest conviction stocks, so that his top 10 picks accounted for approximately 50% of his long portfolio at the end of the second quarter of 2015. He takes a far more patient approach to his longs, which he sometimes holds for years as he waits for an investment thesis to pan out.

For example, Viking began buying stock in the financial company Invesco back in 2007 when it was trading in the mid-$20 range. Halvorsen hung on as it fell below $10 in 2009. But then it began rebounding and Halvorsen eagerly piled on millions of additional shares, becoming the largest shareholder in Invesco. As the stock rose back to the mid-$20 range, Viking finally realized the sizeable gains it foresaw.

Born in Norway, Halvorsen came to the U.S. after his Navy

service to earn his undergraduate degree from Williams College and his MBA from Stanford University before taking up a career in finance and joining Tiger Management.

While his stock picks seem sector agnostic, his selections often match up with those of other Tiger Cubs, all of whom share a common godfather in Robertson.

Below are the holdings of these four managers, and you will note a fair amount of overlap across managers.

FIGURE 49 – BLUE RIDGE 13F CURRENT HOLDINGS AS OF SEPTEMBER 30, 2015; PRICE AS OF NOVEMBER 20, 2015

Company	Symbol	Price	% of Portfolio
Allergan plc	AGN	$312.46	5%
Charter Communications Inc Class /	CHTR	$186.48	5%
Priceline Group Inc	PCLN	$1,281.53	4%
Autodesk Inc	ADSK	$60.55	4%
W. R. Grace & Co	GRA	$98.30	3%
Sensata Technologies Holding NV	ST	$45.75	3%
CDK Global Inc	CDK	$48.51	3%
Endo International PLC	ENDP	$59.37	3%
IHS Inc Class A	IHS	$120.73	3%
Facebook Inc Class A	FB	$107.32	3%

FIGURE 50 – LONE PINE 13F CURRENT HOLDINGS AS OF SEPTEMBER 30, 2015; PRICE AS OF NOVEMBER 20, 2015

Company	Symbol	Price	% of Portfolio
Valeant Pharmaceuticals Internatio	VRX	$91.00	6%
Priceline Group Inc	PCLN	$1,281.53	6%
Charter Communications Inc Class /	CHTR	$186.48	5%
JD.Com Class A	JD	$29.99	5%
Microsoft Corp	MSFT	$54.19	5%
Amazon.com Inc	AMZN	$668.45	4%
Facebook Inc Class A	FB	$107.32	4%
Fleetcor Technologies Inc	FLT	$152.21	4%
MasterCard Inc Class A	MA	$99.50	3%
Equinix	EQIX	$298.60	3%

Company	Symbol	Price	% of Portfolio
Liberty Global PLC Class C	LBTYK	$40.86	9%
Aramark	ARMK	$32.65	8%
Alphabet Inc Class C	GOOG	$756.60	8%
CommScope Holding Company Inc	COMM	$28.30	6%
Sabre Corp	SABR	$29.51	5%
Sensata Technologies Holding NV	ST	$45.75	4%
TransDigm Group Inc	TDG	$236.25	4%
Santander Consumer USA Holdings	SC	$17.56	4%
Anheuser Busch Inbev	BUD	$125.85	4%
Pfizer Inc	PFE	$32.18	4%

FIGURE 52 – VIKING 13F CURRENT HOLDINGS AS OF SEPTEMBER 30, 2015; PRICE AS OF NOVEMBER 20, 2015

Company	Symbol	Price	% of Portfolio
Allergan plc	AGN	$312.46	8%
Walgreens Boots Alliance Inc	WBA	$81.83	7%
Alphabet Inc Class A	GOOGL	$777.00	6%
Amazon.com Inc	AMZN	$668.45	6%
Broadcom Corp Class A	BRCM	$53.53	5%
LyondellBasell Industries NV Class A	LYB	$93.29	4%
Valeant Pharmaceuticals Internatio	VRX	$91.00	3%
Avago Technologies Ltd	AVGO	$126.40	3%
Anthem Inc	ANTM	$131.29	3%
Pioneer Natural Resources Co	PXD	$141.21	3%

Source: AlphaClone

Popularity Screen

Earlier, I discussed picking managers who have different styles and holdings as the best way to build a portfolio. But what if a subset of managers have a very similar style? The Tiger Cubs are often classically similar in that their funds seek high absolute returns by owning shares in businesses with outstanding investment characteristics and selling short the stock of companies with fundamental problems. Investment decisions are based on detailed, company-specific research with a long-term time horizon—the classic valued-added research that many long-short managers strive to employ, but few master. What if, instead of taking the top ten positions from each manager, we just selected the ten most widely held positions across a group of managers?

We include fifteen funds in our analysis below that are referred to as Tiger Cubs, or first generation offspring of the original Tiger operation. There are dozens of other funds that are offspring (Cubs, Grand Cubs, Seeds, etc.) of the original Tiger Management and first-generation funds. (Included funds: Blue Ridge, Coatue, Conatus, Fox Point, Hoplite, Hound, Lone Pine, Maverick, Miura, Second Curve, Tiger Global, Tiger Veda, Valinor, and Viking.)

I looked at the ten most popular positions across the Cubs to see how that portfolio would have performed. Not surprisingly: great!

Note: A popularity screen makes sense for a group of managers like the Tiger Cubs, or some solid value managers. What it doesn't make sense for is the broad hedge fund universe—you end up concentrating in popular names and our research shows that has been a strategy with large underperformance. Novus has also examined investing in popular stocks across the whole hedge fund universe and found that they underperform the broad market by about 3 percent a year. You don't want the beta in hedge funds!

**FIGURE 53 – 13F CURRENT HOLDINGS AS OF SEPTEMBER 30, 2015;
PRICE AS OF NOVEMBER 20, 2015**

Company	Symbol	Price	% of Portfolio
Allergan plc	AGN	$312.46	15%
JD.Com Class A	JD	$29.99	12%
Charter Communications Inc Class /	CHTR	$186.48	12%
Walgreens Boots Alliance Inc	WBA	$81.83	10%
Fleetcor Technologies Inc	FLT	$152.21	10%
Valeant Pharmaceuticals Internatio	VRX	$91.00	9%
Netflix Inc	NFLX	$123.84	9%
Amazon.com Inc	AMZN	$668.45	8%
Facebook Inc Class A	FB	$107.32	8%
Cheniere Energy Inc	LNG	$50.24	8%

FIGURE 54 – 13F PERFORMANCE, 2000–2014

2000-2014	Clone	S&P 500
Return	10.57%	4.31%
Volatility	20.69%	15.24%
Sharpe (1.83%)	0.42	0.16
Drawdown	-48.17%	-50.95%

Year	Clone	S&P 500	Difference
2000	1.7%	-8.2%	9.9%
2001	-1.4%	-11.9%	10.5%
2002	-23.2%	-22.1%	-1.1%
2003	28.0%	28.7%	-0.7%
2004	28.4%	10.9%	17.5%
2005	18.9%	4.9%	14.0%
2006	13.0%	15.8%	-2.8%
2007	45.3%	5.5%	39.8%
2008	-44.5%	-37.0%	-7.5%
2009	60.5%	26.5%	34.0%
2010	4.5%	15.1%	-10.6%
2011	-0.3%	2.1%	-2.4%
2012	28.1%	16.0%	12.1%
2013	43.4%	32.4%	11.0%
2014	7.4%	13.7%	-6.3%

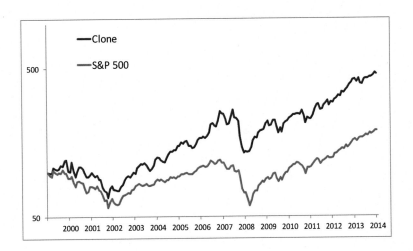

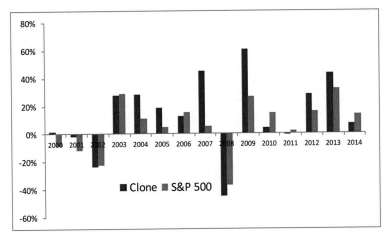

Source: AlphaClone

Here is also a cool visualization matrix from the research shop Novus Partners on the Tiger Cubs, Grand Cubs, and Seeds—and their holdings. While it is difficult to see on the below chart, the website allows the user to view overlapping positions and uniqueness of all the funds. Many are quite similar—spend some time on their website and you can see just how close many of their holdings are.

FIGURE 55 – TIGER MATRIX

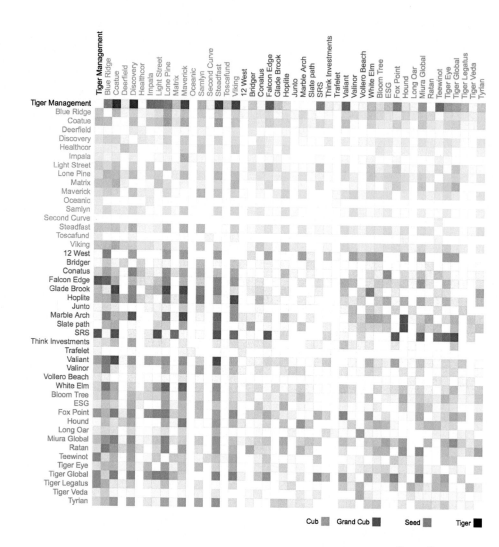

Source: Novus.

CHAPTER 24

HEDGING

While we have examined the results of long-only portfolios, many investors prefer less volatile portfolios. Investors could employ a simple hedging strategy, buying puts or shorting various indices with futures to reduce volatility and market exposure. Below is the same 200-stock portfolio as in the previous chapter, but with hedges in place to run the portfolio at 100 percent hedged (market neutral). Note that no adjustments were made for short interest or margin rates on the futures. Of course the performance of this strategy, and every strategy in this book, rests on the ability of these managers to continue to outperform the indices. 2000 was a particularly easy time to outperform the index as the market-cap-weighted S&P 500 reached the highest valuation on record back to 1880 (as measured by the 10-year cyclically adjusted price-to-earnings ratio (CAPE)). Personally, I would not expect the below simulated returns to be replicable in the future, especially the drawdown figure.

FIGURE 56 – 13F PERFORMANCE, 2000–2014

2000-2014	Clone	S&P 500
Return	9.39%	4.31%
Volatility	6.88%	15.24%
Sharpe (1.83%)	1.10	0.16
Drawdown	-6.65%	-50.95%

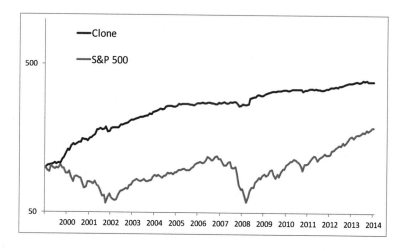

Many readers of my whitepapers and first book, *The Ivy Portfolio*, are familiar with my trend-following studies. A similar hedging approach could be to short the market/hedge out the portfolio when the broad index is below the long-term trend. For more information on this approach, you can read my 2007 whitepaper, "A Quantitative Approach to Tactical Asset Allocation."

CHAPTER 25

SUMMARY

I always like to read research paper or book summaries in bullet format. (Maybe becasue I like to skip to the end.) Hopefully, you have enjoyed the fascinating world of many of these fund managers, and the ideas presented here will be a great starting point for more research and stock ideas. You can always follow along with my favorite ideas on The Idea Farm.

Below we condense the 200+ page book into less than ten bullets:

- It is very simple to track holdings of institutional fund managers using the 13F filings submitted quarterly to the SEC.
- Following a subset of fund managers can lead to new investment ideas. Additionally, investment portfolios can be constructed tracking a hedge fund's long portfolio performance without many of the traditional drawbacks of allocating to private funds.
- Because value managers have long-term holding periods and low turnover, the forty-five-day delay in reported holdings should not be a significant drawback.

- Case studies are presented examining twenty value investors. Backtested results are presented for the portfolios since 2000.
- Results indicate that by tracking and rebalancing portfolios quarterly, an investor can effectively replicate the long holdings of value hedge funds without paying the high hedge fund fees.
- Following the top value hedge funds can result in excess returns with in-line volatility compared with the equity and hedge fund indices.
- An investor could invest in multiple managers to create his or her own fund of funds.
- Additional applications include constructing hedged portfolios, leveraged portfolios, and sector portfolios.

CHAPTER 26

IMPLEMENTATION

We have explored a number of portfolios and approaches in this book, as well as examining twenty fund managers. So how does an investor implement these strategies?

First, an individual investor could track any one manager or build their own "hedge fund of funds" by choosing a group of their favorite managers. If you recall from Chapter 24, we demonstrated that you could replicate most managers with their top five holdings. So even if you follow twenty funds - that is a fairly reasonable list of 100 stocks. (If you exclude the top holding as a suboptimal pick, that reduces the number to 80 stocks.) However, it is very important to pay attention to commissions and spreads that an investor would pay to execute this portfolio. Thankfully, there are a number of brokerages that charge reasonable transaction costs (and plenty that do not!). Some brokerages to explore include Interactive Brokers, Motif, Folio, TD Ameritrade, and Robin Hood.

Some good sites that track 13F holdings include Whale Wisdom and Insider Monkey, and newsletters such as Market Folly and SuperInvestor Insight.

For those that don't want to track and trade 13F strategies

themselves, there are a handful of funds, public and private, that are managed by professional investors tracking 13F strategies. A few companies, such as AlphaClone, Novus, and Global X, manage portfolios through separate accounts, private funds, and ETFs that are based on 13F concepts.

A very enterprising researcher with time on their hands could find a stock database without survivor bias and piece together backtests from publicly available databases. Such resources include Norgate Data, Bloomberg, the SEC, and FactSet. But, be forewarned, it is a tedious process!

AlphaClone previously allowed investors to backtest strategies with their software but made it proprietary to focus on asset management. Whale Wisdom, Symmetric.io, and GuruFocus all have some backtesting capabilities.

Some resources for further exploration are included in the Appendix.

WEBSITES, CONFERENCES, AND READING LISTS

Mebane Faber's Websites

- Meb Faber Research
- The Idea Farm
- Cambria Investment Management
- Cambria Funds

Websites

Below are some great websites for tracking hedge funds as well as finding new investment ideas:

- Alpha Architect
- AlphaClone
- Barron's Roundtable
- Bloomberg Hedge Fund Brief
- cxo Advisory

- DealBook
- Filings Analysis
- Hedge Fund Alert
- Hedge Fund Letters
- Hedge Fund Wisdom
- Insider Monkey
- Insider Score
- Institutional Investor
- J3SG
- Market Folly
- Novus Partners
- SumZero
- SuperInvestor Insight
- Validea
- Value Investing Club
- Whale Wisdom

Conferences

Below is a list of conferences that are a good source of new ideas, roughly in approximate order of the calendar year:

- Wine Retreat
- Ira Sohn
- Value Investing Congress
- Value Conferences
- Drobny
- The Big Picture
- Boston Investment Conference
- Grant's Conference
- Invest for Kids
- Santangels Forum
- Barron's Roundtable
- UVa Investment Conference

- Great Investors' Best Ideas
- Bloomberg Global Summit
- Harbor Investment Conference

Books Profiling Top Hedge Fund Managers

Below is a list of books that profile top hedge fund managers.

- *Hedge Hunters* by Katherine Burton
  - → Yusko, Armitage, Effron, Ainslie, Pickens, Anderson, Robertson, Loeb
- *20/20 Vision* by Harry Liem
  - → Dalio, Inker, Beckers, Mobius, Harding
- *The New Investment Superstars* by Lois Peltz
  - → Ainslie, Cooperman, Griffin, Henry, Tepper, Sussman
- *Market Wizards* by Jack Schwager
  - → Kovner, Dennis, Tudor Jones, Seykota, Steinhardt, Rogers
- *The New Market Wizards* by Jack Schwager
  - → Lipschutz, Eckhardt, Trout, Druckenmiller, Sperandeo, Basso, Hull
- *Inside the House of Money* and *The Invisible Hands* by Steven Drobny
- *Fooling Some of the People All of the Time* by David Einhorn
- *Money Masters of Our Time* by John Train
  - → Buffett, Cabot, Fisher, Graham, Kroll, Price, Templeton, Tisch, Wilson
- *The New Money Masters* by John Train
  - → Soros, Lynch, Neff, Rogers, Caret
- *Investment Gurus* by Peter Tanous
  - → Price, Gabelli, Sharpe, Fama, Sinquefield, D.E. Shaw
- *More Money than God* by Sebastian Mallaby
- *All About Hedge Funds* by Robert Jaeger
- *Absolute Returns* by Alexander Ineichen
- *Handbook of Alternative Investments* by Mark Anson
- *Profiting from Hedge Funds* by John Vincent

Suggested Reading from Top Hedge Fund Managers

Below are a few more reading suggestions from various hedge fund managers:

John Griffin's Recommended Reading List

- *The Art of Short Selling* by Kathryn Staley
- *Financial Shenanigans: How to Detect Accounting Gimmicks* by Howard Schilit
- *A Random Walk Down Wall Street* by Burton Malkiel
- *One Up On Wall Street* by Peter Lynch
- *The Warren Buffett Way* by Robert Hagstrom
- *Security Analysis* by Graham & Dodd
- *Common Stock and Uncommon Profits* by Philip Fisher
- *Winning the Loser's Game: Timeless Strategies for Successful Investing* by Charles Ellis
- *Built to Last: Successful Habits of Visionary Companies* by Collins & Porras
- *Against the Gods* by Peter Bernstein

John Griffin's Behavioral Finance Reading List

- *Investment Psychology Explained: Classic Strategies to Beat the Market* by Martin Pring
- *Beyond Greed and Fear* by Hersh Shefrin
- *The Money Game* by Adam Smith
- *Influence: The Psychology of Persuasion* by Robert Cialdini
- *The Inefficient Stock Market* by Robert Haugen
- *Why Smart People Make Big Money Mistakes* by Gilovich & Belsky
- *The Psychology and Judgment of Decision Making* by Scott Plous
- *How We Know What Isn't So* by Thomas Gilovich
- *Decision Traps: 10 Barriers to Brilliant Decision Making* by J. Russo

- *Extraordinary Popular Delusions and the Madness of Crowds* by Tobias & Mackay
- *Hare Brain, Tortoise Mind* by Guy Claxton
- *The Moral Animal: Why We Are the Way We Are* by Robert Wright
- *How To Win Friends and Influence People* by Dale Carnegie
- *Atlas Shrugged* by Ayn Rand
- *The Tao Jones Averages* by Bennett Goodspeed
- *The Tao of Pooh* by Benjamin Hoff
- *The Te of Piglet* by Benjamin Hoff
- *Nonzero: The Logic of Human Destiny* by Robert Wright
- *The Money Masters* (as well as *The New Money Masters*) both by John Train
- *No Bull* by Michael Steinhardt
- *Soros on Soros: Staying Ahead of the Curve* by George Soros
- *Wall Street: A History* by Charles Geisst
- *Where Are the Customers' Yachts?* by Fred Schwed
- *The New Market Wizards* and *Interviews With Top Traders* both by Jack Schwager
- *Reminiscences of a Stock Operator* by Edwin Lefèvre
- *Classic II: Another Investor's Anthology* by Ellis & Vertin
- *The Great Game* by John S. Gordon
- *Famous First Bubbles* by Peter Garber
- *Chainsaw: The Notorious Career of Al Dunlap* by John Byrne
- *The Essays of Warren Buffett* by Warren Buffett
- *Go-Go Years: Drama and Crashing Finale of Wall Street's Bullish 60s* by John Brooks
- *Baruch: My Own Story* by Bernard Baruch

Bill Ackman's Reading List

- *Security Analysis* by Benjamin Graham
- *One Up on Wall Street* by Peter Lynch
- *Quality of Earnings* by Thornton O'Glove
- *The Essays of Warren Buffett* by Warren Buffett
- *The Intelligent Investor* by Benjamin Graham

Seth Klarman's Reading List

- *The Intelligent Investor* by Benjamin Graham & Jason Zweig
- *You Can Be a Stock Market Genius* by Joel Greenblatt
- *The Aggressive Conservative Investor* by Martin J. Whitman & Martin Shubik
- *Bernard M. Baruch: The Adventures of a Wall Street Legend* by James Grant
- *Money of the Mind* by James Grant
- *Mr. Market Miscalculates: The Bubble Years and Beyond* by James Grant
- *Buffett: The Making of an American Capitalist* by Roger Lowenstein
- *When Genius Failed: The Rise and Fall of Long-Term Capital Management* by Roger Lowenstein
- *The End of Wall Street* by Roger Lowenstein
- *Moneyball: The Art of Winning an Unfair Game* by Michael Lewis
- *Too Big to Fail* by Andrew Ross Sorkin

David Einhorn's Reading List

- *You Can Be a Stock Market Genius* by Joel Greenblatt
- *Margin of Safety* by Seth Klarman
- *Liar's Poker* by Michael Lewis
- *Fooling Some of the People All of the Time* by David Einhorn

Warren Buffett's Reading List

- *Common Stocks and Uncommon Profits* by Phil Fisher
- *The Smartest Guys in the Room* by Bethany McLean
- *The Intelligent Investor* by Benjamin Graham
- *John Bogle on Investing: The First 50 Years* by John Bogle
- *The Essays of Warren Buffett* by Warren Buffett & edited by Larry Cunningham
- *Sam Walton: Made in America* by Sam Walton
- *The Outsiders: Eight Unconventional CEOs and Their Radically Rational Blueprint for Success* by William N. Thorndike
- *Tap Dancing to Work: Warren Buffett on Practically Everything* by Carol Loomis
- *The Clash of Cultures: Investment vs Speculation* by Jack Bogle
- *Investing Between the Lines: How to Make Smarter Decisions By Decoding CEO Communications* by Laura Rittenhouse

Third Point Hedge Fund Manager Daniel Loeb's Reading List

- *Reminiscences of a Stock Operator* by Edwin Lefèvre
- *You Can Be a Stock Market Genius* by Joel Greenblatt
- *Financial Shenanigans: How to Detect Accounting Gimmicks & Fraud* by Howard Schilit
- *The Art of Short Selling* by Kathryn Staley
- *The Power of Story* by Jim Loehr

ABRAMS CAPITAL MANAGEMENT, DAVID ABRAMS

David Abrams tends to let his actions speak for themselves. Rarely quoted, he quietly goes about his business at his Boston-based firm, Abrams Capital Management, which has about $8 billion in assets. Fortunately for Abrams, his actions speak volumes about his skill as an investor.

Since its founding in 1999, Abrams Capital boasts average annualized returns in its main funds of about 15 percent, double the average for hedge funds tracked by HFR Inc. and about triple the S&P 500 index. Even more impressively, Abrams reaches those numbers using virtually no leverage and frequently holding significant portions of his portfolios in cash. He once commented that he has so much dislike of leverage that he carries no personal mortgages.

A graduate of the University of Pennsylvania with a degree in history, Abrams started out in merger arbitrage and bond trading before joining Baupost in 1988. About a decade later he left to form his own firm. While he is known for his skill as a stock picker, he also invests in debt and has sometimes dabbled in real estate.

Abrams runs a concentrated portfolio with most of his invested capital tied up in his top five or six picks. As of the third quarter of 2015, he held over 50 percent of his portfolio in just four names, including Western Union, Wells Fargo, Microsoft, and Barnes & Noble.

FIGURE 57 – 13F CURRENT HOLDINGS AS OF SEPTEMBER 30, 2015; PRICE AS OF NOVEMBER 20, 2015

Company	Symbol	Price	% of Portfolio
Western Union Co	WU	$19.06	28%
Microsoft Corp	MSFT	$54.19	16%
Wells Fargo & Co	WFC	$55.82	10%
Barnes & Noble Education Inc	BNED	$14.85	7%
Barnes & Noble Inc	BKS	$12.78	6%
Opus Bank	OPB	$37.48	6%
Manitowoc Company Inc	MTW	$16.33	5%
Cleco Corp	CNL	$49.40	5%
Interxion Holding NV	INXN	$30.30	5%
Global Eagle Entertainment Inc	ENT	$10.57	4%

Source: AlphaClone.

Abrams is not just a devotee of the investing style pioneered by Benjamin Graham and Warren Buffett, but he believes there is just about no other way to consistently make money in the markets.

"I've actually never seen people be successful over a long period of time without being value investors," Abrams said at one of his rare public appearances, an investment symposium at Columbia University in 1988. "All things equal, the lower the price of something, you have both less risk and more return. And people either get that instantaneously or they don't. The good news…is that most people just never get it, which is really what keeps us in business."

While Abrams prefers to shop for bargain prices when he invests, that does not mean he buys companies that are terminally ill. What he seeks are companies with sound fundamentals but that may not be recognized as good buys by Wall Street. "Good jockeys will do well on good horses, but not on broken down nags," Abrams once said at Wharton Investment Management Club's Speaker Series.

Abrams finds his bargains in both well-known companies and obscure ones. One consistent theme is that if he finds a company he likes, he hangs on to it for a long time, often for years.

Abrams' adherence to value principles extends to his own firm, which he runs with minimal staffing or external marketing. Like some other wealthy hedge fund managers, Abrams owns a piece of a professional sports team. But in Abrams' case, it is a deep value investment—the Oakland Raiders (I'm a Broncos fan!).

So how have his picks performed?

FIGURE 58 – 13F PERFORMANCE, FEBRUARY 2002–2014

2/2002-2014	Clone	S&P 500
Return	13.39%	6.84%
Volatility	20.78%	14.76%
Sharpe (1.41%)	0.58	0.37
Drawdown	-63.55%	-50.95%

Year	Clone	S&P 500	Difference
2000			
2001			
2002			
2003	39.2%	28.7%	10.5%
2004	27.9%	10.9%	17.0%
2005	15.8%	4.9%	10.9%
2006	19.7%	15.8%	3.9%
2007	-0.9%	5.5%	-6.4%
2008	-46.5%	-37.0%	-9.5%
2009	65.0%	26.5%	38.5%
2010	53.5%	15.1%	38.4%
2011	7.7%	2.1%	5.6%
2012	20.7%	16.0%	4.7%
2013	23.6%	32.4%	-8.8%
2014	16.5%	13.7%	2.8%

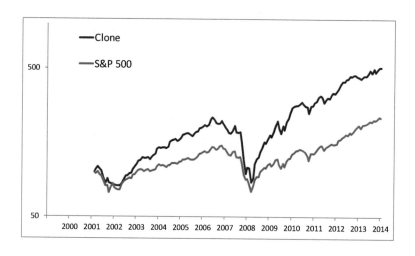

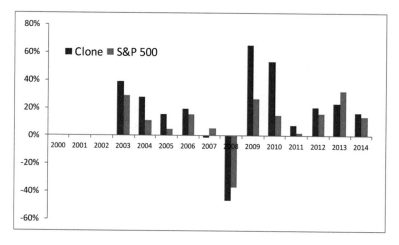

Source: AlphaClone.

AKRE CAPITAL MANAGEMENT, CHUCK AKRE

Successful money managers often have trophy works of art adorning their offices. Charles T. Akre has a nineteenth-century wooden milking stool. It's there to make a point about his investment style.

Akre is the founder, CEO, and chief investment officer of Akre Capital Management, which runs more than $4 billion in mutual fund and hedge fund vehicles. Akre started out as retail broker at Johnston Lemon & Co. in 1968 after earning a degree in English literature from American University. He formed Akre Capital in 1989 and then joined with Friedman, Billings & Ramsey to launch the FBR Small Cap mutual fund. He left Friedman in 1999 and reestablished Akre Capital Management as an independent firm in 2000.

He practices a style of investing that combines value and growth and revolves around stock picking based on a system that he likes to call a three-legged stool.

First, he looks for companies with high return on capital and strong pricing power—fundamentally sound companies rather than ones with serious issues. Then he checks for managers who cater to the interests of shareholders. Finally, he reviews how free cash flow is used, looking for profitable reinvestment practices.

Akre is a highly skeptical analyst, wary of how business managers will deploy capital placed with them by investors. As he once said, "We want to invest not only in highly capable managers, but also those with clear track records of integrity and acting in shareholders' best interest. I've found that when a manager puts his hands in shareholders' pockets once, he's much more likely to do it again."

There is, of course, a final consideration before Akre buys a stock, and that is the price. Once he has a company in his sights, "We apply our sophisticated valuation methodology, which is basically, 'We're not willing to pay very much.'"

Akre typically holds favored positions for long periods, and he tends to run a concentrated portfolio with thirty-five to forty positions, but with assets heavily concentrated in his top five picks. While he has sometimes been characterized as having a focus on mid-sized companies, his picks can range from the very large—Apple, for example—to the very small, such as Diamond Hill Investment Group, an investment advisor that had a market cap of less than $300 million when he owned it.

What has Akre owned lately?

FIGURE 59 – 13F CURRENT HOLDINGS AS OF SEPTEMBER 30, 2015; PRICE AS OF NOVEMBER 20, 2015

Company	Symbol	Price	% of Portfolio
American Tower	AMT	$100.49	13%
MasterCard Inc Class A	MA	$99.50	10%
Markel Corp	MKL	$900.47	10%
Moody's Corp	MCO	$104.34	8%
Dollar Tree Inc	DLTR	$68.42	7%
Roper Technologies Inc	ROP	$191.49	5%
Colfax Corp	CFX	$27.07	5%
O'Reilly Automotive Inc	ORLY	$270.50	5%
Carmax Inc	KMX	$57.41	4%
Visa Inc Class A	V	$80.19	4%

FIGURE 60 – 13F PERFORMANCE, 2/2001 - 2014

2/2001-2014	Clone	S&P 500
Return	15.48%	5.04%
Volatility	20.85%	15.16%
Sharpe (1.52%)	0.67	0.23
Drawdown	-55.01%	-50.95%

Year	Clone	S&P 500	Difference
2000			
2001			
2002	-9.1%	-22.1%	13.0%
2003	68.0%	28.7%	39.3%
2004	37.0%	10.9%	26.1%
2005	3.7%	4.9%	-1.2%
2006	29.3%	15.8%	13.5%
2007	-2.1%	5.5%	-7.6%
2008	-41.1%	-37.0%	-4.1%
2009	68.3%	26.5%	41.8%
2010	22.4%	15.1%	7.3%
2011	21.5%	2.1%	19.4%
2012	16.8%	16.0%	0.8%
2013	44.0%	32.4%	11.6%
2014	5.7%	13.7%	-8.0%

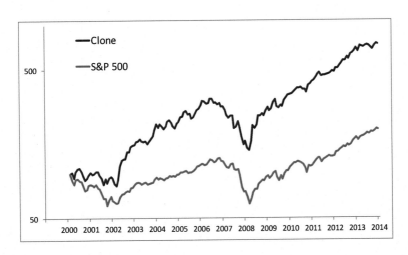

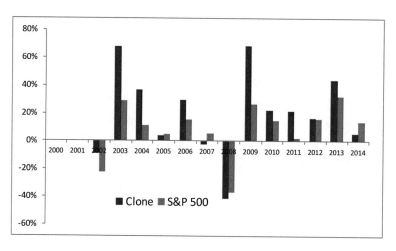

Source: AlphaClone.

These days a photo of the three-legged stool is the main image on the Akre home page. It is a fitting metaphor for the home-spun investing style Akre continues to practice today. He lists Will Rogers as an inspiration, and points to a quip from the Oklahoma-bred humorist as a useful guide. As Rogers once said, "Don't gamble. Take all your savings and buy some good stock and hold it till it goes up, then sell it. If it don't go up, don't buy it."

That pretty well sums up the straightforward investing style that Akre practices.

CANNELL CAPITAL, J. CARLO CANNELL

When it comes to bombast, few can measure up to J. Carlo Cannell, not even the king of loud equity commentary, Jim Cramer. An activist investor, Cannell took a major stake in TheStreet Inc., the financial information site, and took Cramer to task for simultaneously working for NBC while also being paid by TheStreet Inc., which Cramer co-founded.

Cannell wrote in a letter to the company that Cramer spent too much time holding forth on NBC and was a drain on TheStreet, not only for the hefty salary he drew at TheStreet but also for the perks, including things such as "perfumed sedan driver(s) and assorted assistants who spray ionized lavender water on your barren cranium." [23]

Those sorts of barbs are not unusual for Cannell, who has been hurling them since launching his hedge fund firm, Cannell Capital, in 1992. The drama that Cannell brings to the boardroom is part of a canny strategy of picking on smaller, off-the-radar companies that he believes can be pushed into mergers, downsizings, management changes, or other actions aimed at enhancing share value. He specializes in small-cap companies with depressed stock prices that have suffered because of some sort of trouble, although sometimes a company is simply overlooked by Wall Street.

"We are always looking for areas of fear and panic," he once said. "It could be an industry-wide problem...It could be a scandal... With some companies, people just panic."

While Cannell has had his ups and downs, his general direction has been up. From 1992 to mid-2006, his main fund at the time, Tonga Partners, earned net annualized returns of 25.2 percent, more than double the Russell 2000.

Cannell plays both sides of the equity game and is an active short seller of companies. His assets under management have been variously estimated as between $700 million to $800 million, although his long positions appear to account for less than half the total. His portfolio is skewed toward his top fifteen to twenty positions; his recent reported holdings showed more than sixty-one total.

Cannell comes from a family of investors (both his father and grandfather ran investment firms). After earning a degree in sociology from Princeton University, he worked as a freelance journalist in Fiji, then got his business degree from Templeton College at Oxford University in England. He worked at Dakin Securities in San Francisco before leaving to form Cannell Capital in 1992.

Operating now from Jackson, Wyoming, Cannell continues to hunt for small, overlooked companies trading at what his research suggests are substantial discounts. He continues to take active roles in companies where he holds a major stake, and when he doesn't get his way, he tends to complain loudly.

In 2014, he took the management of ValueVision Media to task for spending $3 million on public relations and legal work to fight a request for a special shareholder meeting. "Did you really need to waste our money like that?" he asked in a letter to the board.[24]

Sometimes Cannell's appearance as a major investor in a company can cause a brief move up in the stock price. Sometimes his loud protestations can lead to changes that enhance value. And sometimes nothing seems to work, and Cannell is left to bide his time and hope his investment someday pans out. That appears to be the case with TheStreet.

The company was trading for $16 in December 2007 before crashing in 2008 to $2. It has been hovering in the $1.75 to $3 range ever since. Cannell's suggestion that Cramer quit TheStreet has gone unheeded, as has his push to put the company up for sale. Cannell has been silent since then, but it remains to be seen how long the normally loquacious investor remains that way.

While TheStreet is not a top ten position for Cannell, what holdings is he most invested in now?

FIGURE 61 – 13F CURRENT HOLDINGS AS OF SEPTEMBER 30, 2015; PRICE AS OF NOVEMBER 20, 2015

Company	Symbol	Price	% of Portfolio
GTT Communications Inc	GTT	$20.76	13%
BioTelemetry Inc	BEAT	$12.40	7%
Intralinks Holdings Inc	IL	$10.25	6%
Build-A-Bear Workshop Inc	BBW	$12.16	6%
EVINE Live Inc Class A	EVLV	$ 2.42	5%
TeleCommunication Systems Inc Class A	TSYS	$ 4.39	4%
Regional Management Corp	RM	$15.27	4%
Genesis Healthcare Inc Class A	GEN	$ 4.65	4%
Cavco Industries Inc	CVCO	$91.77	3%
North American Energy Partners Inc	NOA	$ 2.18	3%

Source: AlphaClone

FIGURE 62 – 13F PERFORMANCE, 2001- 2014

2/2001-2014	Clone	S&P 500
Return	16.45%	5.04%
Volatility	25.35%	15.16%
Sharpe (1.52%)	0.59	0.23
Drawdown	-66.51%	-50.95%

Year	Clone	S&P 500	Difference
2000			
2001			
2002	-9.4%	-22.1%	12.7%
2003	42.9%	28.7%	14.2%
2004	32.0%	10.9%	21.1%
2005	14.9%	4.9%	10.0%
2006	28.2%	15.8%	12.4%
2007	25.6%	5.5%	20.1%
2008	-49.1%	-37.0%	-12.1%
2009	21.3%	26.5%	-5.2%
2010	29.3%	15.1%	14.2%
2011	0.8%	2.1%	-1.3%
2012	19.6%	16.0%	3.6%
2013	96.4%	32.4%	64.0%
2014	30.4%	13.7%	16.7%

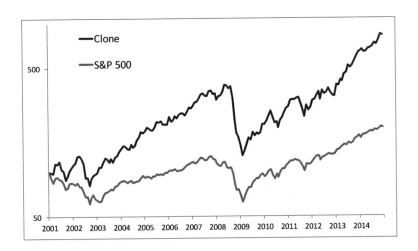

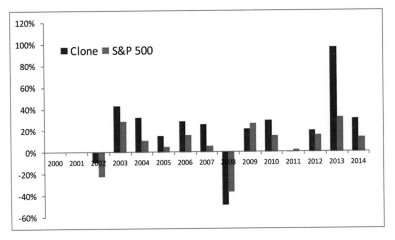

Source: AlphaClone.

THE CHILDREN'S INVESTMENT FUND MANAGEMENT

It's called The Children's Investment Fund Management, but it doesn't have much to do these days with the charity from which it got its name. TCI, as it is now usually called, is the London-based hedge fund managed by Christopher Hohn, and its modus operandi is anything but childish.

Hohn is an activist investor who runs a highly concentrated portfolio and is bent on muscling his way into boardrooms and forcing change. His style has been called "poison," Hohn has been called a "locust," and Hohn himself has said he regularly receives death threats.

"People say to me, 'you're too controversial, you're too directional, you're too concentrated, you take too much risk,'" he said at a Euro-Hedge conference. "I say to them, 'That's all true, but I make money.'"

He makes a lot of it, for both himself and his investors. *Alpha* magazine placed him in a tie for the twenty-second highest-paid hedge fund manager in its 2015 ranking, estimating his take at $180 million.[25] The firm's main fund posted annualized gains of 19.2 percent over the previous five years.

TCI manages about $8 billion and is regarded as one of Britain's largest and most successful hedge funds. It typically holds only a handful of positions at a time, often fewer than a dozen stocks. But its largest positions give Hohn a seat in the corporate board-room. TCI can hold on to those positions for extended periods of time as Hohn agitates for change.

On the company website, TCI says it, "Takes a private equity approach to the public markets," and "creates value by constructive engagement with management." It once forced the resignation of the CEO of the Deutsche Boerse, the German stock exchange, after TCI acquired a large stake. In another move, Hohn sued the government of India for the underpricing of coal by an Indian coal company in which TCI held a major stake.

While it is now regarded as a hedge fund like any other, it started out as an unusual public/private hybrid. Founded in 2003, it was set up to automatically donate a sizeable chunk of its profit to The Children's Investment Fund Foundation, a charity run by Hohn's then-wife, Jamie Cooper-Hohn, and was aimed at helping impoverished children in developing countries. When he and his wife separated in 2014, it resulted in one of the biggest divorce cases ever in London. Hohn not only split from his wife, but also severed ties between his hedge fund and her charity.

Hohn grew up in England, the son of a transplanted Jamaican auto mechanic. He went to Harvard Business School, then worked for Perry Capital before leaving to found TCI. The hedge fund started strong but got slammed in the market collapse, losing 43 percent in 2008. It took several years for Hohn to get his groove back, but he is once again on top. His main fund was up 21 percent for the first six months of 2015.

Hohn professes to reach his high-octane returns with much less drama than he used to. He has taken up yoga, given up meat, and has been known to drive a Prius. And he says, he is much more likely to offer constructive criticism to corporate executives than harsh demands.

Judging from his recent returns, the approach appears to be working.

FIGURE 63 – 13F CURRENT HOLDINGS AS OF SEPTEMBER 30, 2015;
PRICE AS OF NOVEMBER 20, 2015

Company	Symbol	Price	% of Portfolio
Time Warner Cable Inc	TWC	$184.00	59%
Comcast Corp	CMCSA	$62.62	23%
Moody's Corp	MCO	$103.43	8%
American Express Co	AXP	$72.74	6%
Baidu Inc	BIDU	$207.80	4%
Ambac Financial Group Inc	AMBC	$15.20	1%

Source: AlphaClone.

FIGURE 64 – 13F PERFORMANCE, 6/2006–2014

6/2006-2014	Clone	S&P 500
Return	19.34%	7.62%
Volatility	21.24%	15.53%
Sharpe (1.06%)	0.86	0.42
Drawdown	-51.55%	-50.95%

Year	Clone	S&P 500	Difference
2000			
2001			
2002			
2003			
2004			
2005			
2006			
2007	5.3%	5.5%	-0.2%
2008	-38.1%	-37.0%	-1.1%
2009	75.1%	26.5%	48.6%
2010	14.2%	15.1%	-0.9%
2011	9.5%	2.1%	7.4%
2012	33.1%	16.0%	17.1%
2013	63.0%	32.4%	30.6%
2014	17.2%	13.7%	3.5%

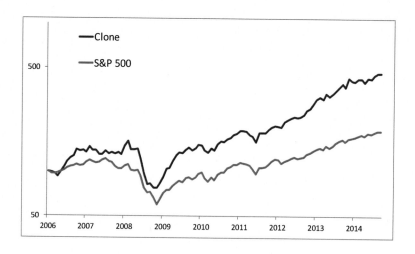

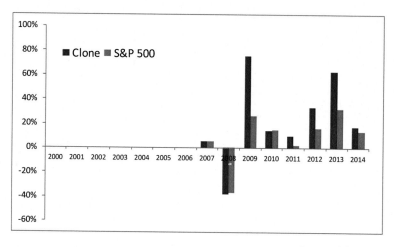

Source: AlphaClone.

DARUMA ASSET MANAGEMENT, MARIKO GORDON

Mariko Gordon likes to play by the rules—her rules. At her Daruma Asset Management, she has distilled her investment process to a set of carefully defined rules that govern stock selection, portfolio concentration and diversification, and holding periods. Sticking to those rules has produced solid returns year after year, handily beating the benchmark Russell 2000 Index.

One key to her success is that she focuses on companies that stand to benefit from some sort of catalyst—a change that has the potential to boost the bottom line. Often the catalyst is some external shift in the business landscape. The trick is identifying the change and the company that stands to benefit. While she hunts for value-priced stocks, she doesn't let price discourage her if she sees significant upside potential.

"The best time to buy is not just when a stock offers good value but when we can also clearly define what might drive the share price higher—which in most cases is better-then-expected sales, earnings, or cash-flow growth," she says.

In some cases, the catalyst is simply a change in leadership. For example, Daruma started buying Gardner Denver, which makes industrial compressors and pumps, in late 2008 at around $30 a share after the company hired a new CEO. That CEO happened to be someone who was coming from another company that Daruma had invested in with good success. Gordon figured the CEO could engineer something similar at Gardner Denver. By the end of 2009, it was trading over $30. When the company was taken private in 2013, its stock was trading around $75.

Today, Daruma manages over $2.3 billion but it continues to maintain a focus on small-cap stocks where a small change in a company or business can make a big difference in the bottom line. This is not a bad accomplishment in the financial world for someone who once thought she might be a writer, an academic, or possibly a journalist.

Gordon was a comparative literature major at Princeton. She went to high school in Hawaii, where she was a classmate of future president Barack Obama. She decided literature or writing probably wouldn't be very lucrative, so she took an entry-level position at an investment firm where she learned the basics of analyzing corporate data like cash flow and working capital (she took night classes on finance to help her get up to speed). She then moved Royce & Associates, where she became immersed in small-cap stocks under her boss, Charles Ross, a small-cap investing icon. She left in 1995 to launch Daruma.

Daruma looks for stocks that it believes have a potential for 50 percent appreciation over two years. It holds twenty-five to thirty-five positions at a time and likes to start a position by initially buying up enough to account for 2 percent of its portfolio, but it limits a full position to no more than 6 percent. The top ten holdings account for 35 to 40 percent of the portfolio. There are a few sectors that she tries to avoid: real estate investment trusts, biotechs, and utilities.

What Gordon wants are smaller public companies that have an opportunity to grow with a few strategic changes in operations or personnel or as a result of some other catalyst.

"Our strategy is particularly tailored to small-caps," she says. "Simpler business models are easier to analyze and cross-check, while at the same time change happens faster in small companies, making for more investable inflection points. One or two people can also make a big difference."

While we don't have a backtest history for the fund, you can find the holdings below.

FIGURE 65 – 13F CURRENT HOLDINGS AS OF SEPTEMBER 30, 2015; PRICE AS OF NOVEMBER 20, 2015

Company	Symbol	Price	% of Portfolio
Acxiom Corporation	ACXM	$21.96	4%
Cadence Design Systems Inc.	CDNS	$21.47	4%
Brunswick Corporation	BC	$54.66	4%
Electronics for Imaging	EFII	$49.00	4%
Beacon Roofing Supply, Inc.	BECN	$37.89	4%
Entegris, Inc.	ENTG	$13.19	3%
HEALTHSOUTH Corp	HLS	$35.16	3%
Texas Capital BancShares	TCBI	$59.15	3%
Diebold, Inc	DBD	$37.51	3%
Constant Contact, Inc.	CTCT	$31.60	3%

Source: Whale Wisdom

ESL INVESTMENTS INC., EDDIE LAMPERT

There are value investors who prefer concentrated portfolios with a small number of high-conviction companies. Then there is Eddie Lampert, who puts that strategy on steroids.

In the first quarter of 2015, Lampert's RBS Partners held a portfolio of just seven positions, and many of those were related. Sears Holdings represented about half of his $2.1 billion worth of invested assets. Lampert serves as chairman and CEO of Sears and also has a sizeable chunk of his personal wealth tied up in the company's stock. Three other RBS positions at the time—Lands End, Gap, and Sears Hometown and Outlet Stores—are Sears spinoffs.

Lampert's love affair with troubled retailer Sears has left many analysts and investors scratching their heads. In a 2013 article, *Forbes* magazine suggested a new nickname for the once-heralded value investor: Wrong Way Lampert.

Lampert remains undeterred, convinced he will ultimately be proven right at Sears. In a blog he posted on the Sears website in May, 2014, Lampert wrote, "Turnarounds are challenging, but transformations are even harder because not everyone sees the direction you're heading in or your destination."

Lampert has always been iconoclastic in his approach and often made a killing thanks to it. Back in 2004, *Bloomberg Businessweek* magazine ran a lengthy profile of him that dubbed him "the next Warren Buffet." At the time, his investment vehicle, ESL (which manages RBS), had returned an average of 29 percent per year since its founding in 1988.

He performed so well in 2004 that his personal take landed him atop the Rich List of hedge fund managers published by *Institutional Investor's Alpha* magazine, which reported that he was the first hedge fund manager to earn more than a billion dollars in a single year.

His headlong foray into Kmart and then Sears has been a bumpy ride. Kmart started out as a big-time distressed debt play. He bought the $23 billion retail chain out of bankruptcy in 2003 for around $1 billion, which gave him access to its generous cash flow and helped fuel his takeover of Sears in 2004.

The Sears gambit has had numerous downs since then and prompted a number of his fund investors to jump ship. But it has also had a few significant ups. Sears stock jumped 18.6 percent in 2013, a year when Lampert also scored with AutoNation, which gained 25.2 percent, and Gap, which rose 25.9 percent. Those gains were enough to earn Lampert a spot at number 14 on the *Alpha* Rich List with a take that year estimated at $400 million.

Lampert wasn't always such a singularly minded investor. He started out in the arbitrage department at Goldman Sachs after graduating from Yale in 1984 with a degree in economics. He left Goldman in 1988 to form ESL when he was 25 years old and practiced a value investing approach not nearly as concentrated as it would later become.

Somehow things seem to turn out in Lampert's favor despite challenges. In 2003, when he was deep into his bid to take control of Kmart, he was kidnapped by four hoods while leaving his office in Connecticut. Held for ransom in a motel room bathtub, Lampert convinced them that he would pay them $40,000 if they let him go. They did, he called the cops, and then went back and completed the Kmart deal.

Company	Symbol	Price	% of Portfolio
Sears Holdings Corp	SHLD	$19.96	34%
AutoNation Inc	AN	$63.43	27%
Lands End Inc	LE	$22.54	12%
Sears Canada Inc	SRSC	$ 8.21	12%
Gap Inc	GPS	$26.98	8%
International Business Machines Cc	IBM	$138.50	4%
Sears Hometown and Outlet Stores	SHOS	$ 7.97	3%
SERITAGE GROWTH PPTYS	SRG	$33.84	1%

Source: AlphaClone.

FIGURE 67 – 13F PERFORMANCE, 2000–2014

2000-2014	Clone	S&P 500
Return	10.15%	4.31%
Volatility	28.45%	15.24%
Sharpe (1.83%)	0.29	0.16
Drawdown	-71.63%	-50.95%

Year	Clone	S&P 500	Difference
2000	20.3%	-8.2%	28.5%
2001	33.4%	-11.9%	45.3%
2002	-16.3%	-22.1%	5.8%
2003	13.7%	28.7%	-15.0%
2004	77.2%	10.9%	66.3%
2005	17.4%	4.9%	12.5%
2006	34.5%	15.8%	18.7%
2007	-22.6%	5.5%	-28.1%
2008	-42.2%	-37.0%	-5.2%
2009	45.3%	26.5%	18.8%
2010	31.5%	15.1%	16.4%
2011	-3.1%	2.1%	-5.2%
2012	17.2%	16.0%	1.2%
2013	2.0%	32.4%	-30.4%
2014	0.8%	13.7%	-12.9%

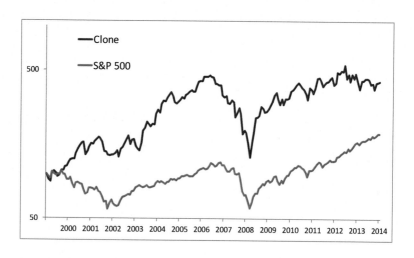

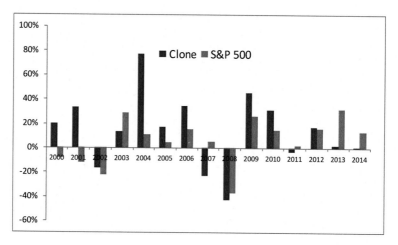

Source: AlphaClone.

FAIRHOLME FUNDS, BRUCE BERKOWITZ

"At some price, a great business becomes a speculation."
— BRUCE BERKOWITZ

Back in 2011, few investors wanted to touch Bank of America or American International Group, two companies battered in the financial meltdown. Bruce Berkowitz could hardly buy enough. He loaded up and patiently waited. Two years later, as both companies proved they were survivors, Berkowitz's bets soared in value.

"With the type of value investing I do, you look very wrong until you're right," Berkowitz says.

Berkowitz tends to come out looking right a lot. His Fairholme Capital, which runs mutual funds and a hedge fund, has been a leading money manager for years. The signature Fairholme Fund (about $5 billion in assets in late 2015), returned more than 450 percent from its inception in 1999 through 2013, compared to about 65 percent for the S&P 500. *Institutional Investor* magazine named him Money Manager of the Year for 2014, while Morningstar crowned him Domestic Equity Manager of the Decade in 2010.

Berkowitz does it by sticking to his style of value investing with concentrated positions and a long-term view. He tends toward old-economy companies like banks and financial firms rather than emerging fields like high-tech. He has taken big positions in Citigroup, Goldman Sachs, and Morgan Stanley, for example. AIG and Bank of America were still his top two holdings at the start of 2014. Several other top positions had been in his portfolio for years, often purchased during particularly difficult times for the companies.

If Berkowitz seems to excel at beating the odds, it may be because he has a special understanding of them. Growing up in Chelsea, Massachusetts, he watched his father run a bookmaking operation out of a convenience store. When he was 15, his father had a heart attack, and young Berkowitz took over the bookmaking operation until his father recovered. Berkowitz maintains that the lessons he learned about odds and how people play them informs his decisions to this day. "I learned hope and dreams and the perverse psychology that makes people make stupid decisions," he says.

After graduating from the University of Massachusetts at Amherst, he moved to London for a job with a consulting group, then on to a job at Merrill Lynch and then Lehman Brothers, which brought him back to the United States. He switched to Salomon Smith Barney before launching Fairholme in December 1999, which soon gained stature as a top-performing mutual fund company.

Berkowitz moved Fairholme from Short Hills, New Jersey, to Miami in 2006, and in 2007, he hired Charlie Fernandez, who had married Berkowitz's cousin, as his second-in-command. The two lived next door to each other and operated Fairholme as a closely allied duo, steering it through the economic collapse.

The odds seemed to finally catch up with Berkowitz in 2011, when his Fairholme Fund lost 32 percent, dragged down by some of his pet long-term investments like AIG, Bank of America, and Sears. In a letter to his investors in 2006, Berkowitz wrote, "Periods of volatility and stress sometimes allow what we buy cheap to become cheaper, creating unusual opportunity. Fairholme's history includes many instances of short-term 'embarrassment' leading to long-term 'victory.'"

The fine line between an embarrassing investment and the victory of high returns is something Berkowitz knows intimately. Fernandez resigned amidst the turmoil. Berkowitz's response: buy more of the same and increase the portfolio concentration. By November 2013, those stocks came roaring back, and the fund was up 37 percent.

Berkowitz was also a major investor in Fannie Mae and Freddie Mac when they were at their worst following the economic meltdown and through their bailout by the federal government. He has battled with the government over its control of the two mortgage giants and revived profits once they started to recover, filing lawsuits and at one point in 2014 sending angry letters ridiculing the government's position as "total nonsense."

Through it all, Berkowitz remains committed to the same investing principles and maintaining a stubborn commitment to his picks. Sure, he has down periods, but he cautions against judging him on short-term results rather than long-term outcomes.

"What's not fair is to believe that a manager or a businessperson is in such control of companies that they can control any one-year period or two-year period," Berkowitz said in an interview with *Fortune* magazine. "I've not seen it done." He is also adamant about distinguishing volatility from risk, pointing out that short-term volatility need not entail high risk and that risk is defined precisely in terms of the likelihood of losing capital. Below are Berkowitz's picks, with roughly 60% of the assets concentrated in the top four holdings.

FIGURE 68 – 13F CURRENT HOLDINGS AS OF SEPTEMBER 30, 2015; PRICE AS OF NOVEMBER 20, 2015

Company	Symbol	Price	% of Portfolio
Sears Holdings Corp	SHLD	$19.96	22%
St. Joe Co	JOE	$19.65	17%
Bank of America Corp	BAC	$17.65	16%
Leucadia National Corp	LUK	$18.06	8%
Canadian Natural Resources Ltd	CNQ	$24.69	7%
Citigroup Inc	C	$54.75	6%
SERITAGE GROWTH PPTYS	SRG	$ 0.00	5%
Sears Canada Inc	SRSC	$ 8.21	4%
International Business Machines Cc	IBM	$138.50	4%
NOW Inc	DNOW	$18.37	4%

Source: AlphaClone.

FIGURE 69 – 13F PERFORMANCE, 2000–2014

2000-2014	Clone	S&P 500
Return	8.21%	4.31%
Volatility	22.55%	15.24%
Sharpe (1.83%)	0.28	0.16
Drawdown	-59.33%	-50.95%

Year	Clone	S&P 500	Difference
2000	45.1%	-8.2%	53.3%
2001	-5.9%	-11.9%	6.0%
2002	-3.7%	-22.1%	18.4%
2003	25.5%	28.7%	-3.2%
2004	38.1%	10.9%	27.2%
2005	16.3%	4.9%	11.4%
2006	26.2%	15.8%	10.4%
2007	11.0%	5.5%	5.5%
2008	-38.9%	-37.0%	-1.9%
2009	34.2%	26.5%	7.7%
2010	11.6%	15.1%	-3.5%
2011	-38.4%	2.1%	-40.5%
2012	31.2%	16.0%	15.2%
2013	33.9%	32.4%	1.5%
2014	-11.2%	13.7%	-24.9%

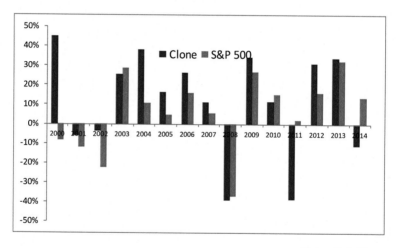

Source: AlphaClone.

GLENVIEW CAPITAL MANAGEMENT, LARRY ROBBINS

Larry Robbins knows a good thing when he sees it. In 2004, he saw a good thing in healthcare stocks, a focus he maintained for the next decade, reaping huge rewards for it.

He first saw profit in healthcare shares after December 2003 when President George W. Bush signed the Medicare Modernization Act, which raised government reimbursements. Robbins started placing big bets on healthcare companies through his Glenview Capital Management. More recently, after Obamacare survived a Supreme Court challenge in 2012, he dove into hospital stocks, figuring hospitals would profit from a rising number of insured patients.

The decade-long focus on healthcare has been a boon for Robbins, particularly in 2013, when *Forbes* magazine said his main hedge fund returned 43 percent net for the year, while the smaller Glenview Opportunities Fund scored a whopping 100 percent return by using leverage and more concentration. Bloomberg Markets named Glenview Opportunities Fund the best-performing large hedge fund for 2013.

Robbins didn't start out to be a specialist in picking healthcare stocks. He founded Glenview in 2001 as a long-short equity shop, with an approach that he says is somewhat akin to the methods employed by Warren Buffett or John Malone (the acquisitive cable magnate). Robbins sums up his approach with the line, "Think like an owner, not like a trader."

Robbins likes to hold positions for years rather than trading in and out of markets. And while he has maintained a passion for healthcare shares, his investments have included a wide range of companies and industries, including General Motors, American International Group, Flextronics, and Xerox.

Robbins' emergence as a top hedge fund manager is in some ways surprising. He says he didn't know what a hedge fund was when he started out in finance.

Robbins grew up outside Chicago and earned simultaneous bachelor's degrees in systems engineering and in marketing, finance, and accounting from the University of Pennsylvania. He went to work in an investment bank in New York and then got hired at Leon Cooperman's hedge fund, Omega Advisors, where he developed and honed his skill researching, analyzing, and investing in equities while working alongside the legendary stock picker Cooperman.

An avid sports fan, Robbins frequently makes allusions to athletics in his presentations. When he left Omega and launched his hedge fund in 2001, he named it after Glenview, Illinois, the town where he played hockey in his youth.

His rise to prominence has not been without its setbacks. After building his assets to more than $9 billion, he saw them shrivel to less than $3 billion in the wake of the financial collapse in 2008, as he suffered investment losses and withdrawals by his investors. But he has rebounded since then, and his assets stood at more than $19 billion again as of March 2015.

In a presentation at the annual Ira Sohn investment conference in 2014, he offered up his views on the markets and some specific stock picks, as well what it takes to successfully play the markets. One of his key points: watch fundamentals closely, and "ignore crowd noise."

In 2014, the crowd was cheering Robbins on for his considerable success playing the markets. But Robbins is the first to acknowledge that such success can be fleeting. "The road from market genius to village idiot is exceedingly short," he quipped.

FIGURE 70 – 13F CURRENT HOLDINGS AS OF SEPTEMBER 30, 2015; PRICE AS OF NOVEMBER 20, 2015

Company	Symbol	Price	% of Portfolio
Humana Inc	HUM	$167.61	6%
Monsanto Co	MON	$96.09	6%
Thermo Fisher Scientific Inc	TMO	$137.84	5%
AbbVie Inc	ABBV	$61.11	4%
Flextronics International Ltd	FLEX	$11.24	4%
Cigna Corp	CI	$132.17	3%
Tenet Healthcare Corp	THC	$31.33	3%
Aetna Inc	AET	$104.43	3%
Anthem Inc	ANTM	$131.29	3%
Laboratory Corporation of America	LH	$121.47	3%

Source: AlphaClone.

FIGURE 71 – 13F PERFORMANCE, 2000–2014

2/2002-2014	Clone	S&P 500
Return	12.30%	6.89%
Volatility	18.93%	14.76%
Sharpe (1.41%)	0.58	0.37
Drawdown	-43.36%	-50.95%

Year	Clone	S&P 500	Difference
2000			
2001			
2002	-35.7%	-22.1%	-13.6%
2003	51.4%	28.7%	22.7%
2004	56.8%	10.9%	45.9%
2005	11.0%	4.9%	6.1%
2006	8.5%	15.8%	-7.3%
2007	27.8%	5.5%	22.3%
2008	-34.6%	-37.0%	2.4%
2009	25.1%	26.5%	-1.4%
2010	7.2%	15.1%	-7.9%
2011	-8.4%	2.1%	-10.5%
2012	32.8%	16.0%	16.8%
2013	45.3%	32.4%	12.9%
2014	22.7%	13.7%	9.0%

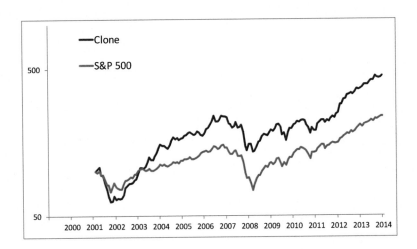

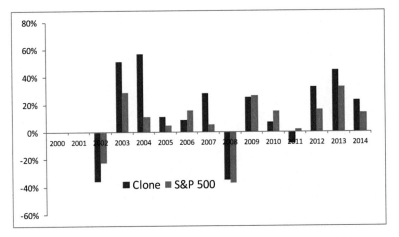

Source: AlphaClone.

ICAHN ENTERPRISES, CARL ICAHN

"I make money. Nothing wrong with that. That's what I do. That's what I want to do. That's what I'm here to do. That's what I enjoy."

— CARL ICAHN

Carl Icahn refuses to retire. The legendary Wall Street activist with the scruffy gray beard and a look that seems to project perpetual disdain has been barging into corporate boardrooms for decades, using his investment clout to demand big changes that result in big profits for him and investors who tag along.

The *New York Times* ran a profile of him in 2011 titled, "The Raider in Winter: Carl Icahn at 75." [26] By 2015 he was pushing 80 and still agitating corporate management. By then he had moved into what should be his grandchildren's territory, Silicon Valley, where he was busy shaking up the likes of Apple, eBay and Netflix.

"What else would I do?" he told *The Times*. "Play shuffleboard somewhere?"

These days he runs Icahn Enterprises, his main investment vehicle, reportedly manages more than $24 billion. He remains one of the most influential activist investors around. He is also one of the most abrasive. There is a saying in corporate America that one of the scariest messages a CEO can receive is that Icahn is calling. In a 2007 interview, Wall Street investor Wilbur Ross said of Icahn, "He is especially good at terrorizing people and wearing down their defenses." [27]

Icahn has always had a knack for spotting a vulnerable CEO, then buying up the company's shares and launching an attack aimed at bending the executive to his will or getting him fired. "CEOs are paid for doing a terrible job," Icahn once said. "If the system wasn't so messed up, guys like me wouldn't make this kind of money."

Icahn may be a billionaire today but he grew up in a modest family in Queens and used poker winnings to help pay his way through Princeton University. He went to medical school but quit before finishing and went into finance on the advice of an uncle. By 1968 he had a seat on the New York Stock Exchange. Soon he was involved in some of the biggest deals of the corporate raider era: RJR Nabisco, TWA, Phillips Petroleum, Time Warner. Some were disasters. But he scored enough mega hits to make himself a billionaire. When Oliver Stone made his movie, *Wall Street,* Icahn was one of several Wall Street investors who were consulted.

Icahn is not just an activist who buys up significant shares of companies and then makes demands on management. He is also a wily opportunist who jumps into situations where he thinks he can extract a quick profit. That's what he did when arch-rival Bill Ackman of Pershing Square laid down his high-profile short of Herbalife, arguing the company was doomed to collapse. Icahn joined hedge fund manager Daniel Loeb in buying up long positions in Herbalife, a move that suddenly drove up the price. To his delight, Icahn not only cashed in but at the same time put a squeeze on Ackman's short play.

Icahn understands the value of his name attached to an investment idea. He is fond of sending "open" letters to corporate management (he penned one in 2014 to Apple CEO Tim Cook) that the press then prints and broadcasts.[28] And he stays up on current trends and methods. He has become an avid user of Twitter.

Icahn's ideas tend to go against the grain, which is how he likes it. Being a contrarian is a mark of pride for him and he sees no reason to change now.

"When most investors, including the pros, all agree on something, they're usually wrong," he says.

For some reason the AlphaClone database only has Icahn's performance back to 2004, which is a much shorter period than he has been managing money. We're only going to include his holdings below, and not the truncated stub period of returns.

FIGURE 72 – 13F CURRENT HOLDINGS AS OF SEPTEMBER 30, 2015; PRICE AS OF NOVEMBER 20, 2015

Company	Symbol	Price	% of Portfolio
Icahn Enterprises LP	IEP	$70.21	28%
Apple Inc	AAPL	$119.30	21%
CVR Energy Inc	CVI	$45.61	11%
PayPal Holdings Inc	PYPL	$36.36	5%
Cheniere Energy Inc	LNG	$50.24	5%
Hologic Inc	HOLX	$40.01	4%
Nuance Communications Inc	NUAN	$20.08	4%
Freeport-McMoRan Inc	FCX	$ 8.25	4%
Federal-Mogul Holdings Corp	FDML	$ 7.62	3%
Herbalife Ltd	HLF	$56.73	3%

Source: AlphaClone.

JANA PARTNERS, BARRY ROSENSTEIN

Barry Rosenstein has opinions about how businesses should be run, and he is not shy about sharing them. As an activist investor, he has pressured companies as varied as the grocery chain Safeway to publisher McGraw-Hill to agricultural supplier Agrium to downsize or split up or take other actions to increase "shareholder value." More often than not, they comply, and Rosenstein walks away richer.

Rosenstein's personal wealth has been estimated at $1.3 billion and his hedge fund, JANA Partners, manages about $11 billion. His personal style tends toward Armani suits and trophy houses, but his investment style is aimed at less flashy companies.

JANA takes a fundamental value approach to its investments, which can include both debt and equity. It looks for firms that it believes contain hidden value that can be unlocked through a catalyst like a downsizing, merger, or sale. On the company website, JANA says it likes to invest "in companies undergoing or expected to undergo change."

Often, that change is initiated by Rosenstein himself, who

makes his wishes known after taking a major position in a company. He moves with the bluster and confidence of one used to getting his way. "I always say to the CEO, 'You could take our ideas and make them your own and be the change agent. The alternative is you could fight us, but you're going to end up in the same place anyway.'"

Rosenstein convinced McGraw-Hill to sell its education business, and the company's shares rose 30 percent in 2013. He pushed Oil States International to spin off a business that builds worker housing, and the stock rose 42 percent.

Just how in-your-face Rosenstein gets depends on the situation. *Barron's* magazine once described his approach as "velvet glove." But in a *Wall Street Journal* article, he was quoted as saying he once intimidated an opponent so thoroughly that he threw up in a meeting.

Rosenstein graduated from Lehigh University and got his MBA from the University of Pennsylvania's Wharton School of Business. He worked his way up on Wall Street, starting in the investment banking unit of Merrill Lynch, then learning the activist game at Plaza Securities, the company run by Asher Edelman, who was a model for the corporate raider Gordon Gekko in the movie *Wall Street*. Rosenstein made a few more stops before launching JANA Partners in 2001 with the financial backing of hedge fund superstar Leon Cooperman.

Being an activist means Rosenstein's bets tend to be concentrated on a few high-conviction stocks, and he will often hold those positions for an extended period of time as he tries to bring about change that will increase value. While that increased value can be a good thing for shareholders, it may not always be as pleasant for the company's workforce—his recommendations can lead to downsizing and significant layoffs.

Rosenstein tended to place a good deal of emphasis on company management ("follow the jockey, not the horse"), although he has shifted somewhat over time, paying more attention to cash flow and other metrics. "We're still very focused on the jockey, but we're equally focused on the cash the businesses produce. In cases where we can't find an absolute superb jockey, we'll still invest if the cash flow is there..."

So where is he finding the cash flow now?

FIGURE 73 – 13F CURRENT HOLDINGS AS OF SEPTEMBER 30, 2015; PRICE AS OF NOVEMBER 20, 2015

Company	Symbol	Price	% of Portfolio
Qualcomm Inc	QCOM	$49.62	18%
ConAgra Foods Inc	CAG	$40.85	14%
Walgreens Boots Alliance Inc	WBA	$81.83	13%
Hertz Global Holdings Inc	HTZ	$16.55	8%
Allergan plc	AGN	$312.46	6%
Computer Sciences Corp	CSC	$69.79	5%
Time Warner Cable Inc	TWC	$184.50	5%
Baxter International Inc	BAX	$38.31	5%
Microsoft Corp	MSFT	$54.19	4%
Liberty Interactive Corp Series A	QVCA	$26.31	4%

Source: AlphaClone.

FIGURE 74 – 13F PERFORMANCE, 2/2003–2014

2/2003-2014	Clone	S&P 500
Return	16.07%	9.87%
Volatility	20.66%	13.98%
Sharpe (1.39%)	0.71	0.61
Drawdown	-59.90%	-50.95%

Year	Clone	S&P 500	Difference
2000			
2001			
2002			
2003			
2004	26.8%	10.9%	15.9%
2005	15.1%	4.9%	10.2%
2006	20.9%	15.8%	5.1%
2007	-0.6%	5.5%	-6.1%
2008	-47.7%	-37.0%	-10.7%
2009	39.2%	26.5%	12.7%
2010	30.6%	15.1%	15.5%
2011	6.2%	2.1%	4.1%
2012	45.2%	16.0%	29.2%
2013	34.1%	32.4%	1.7%
2014	6.0%	13.7%	-7.7%

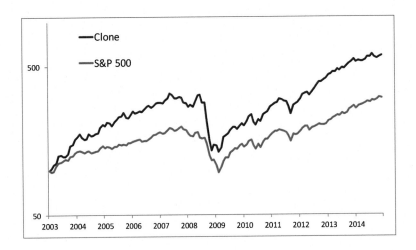

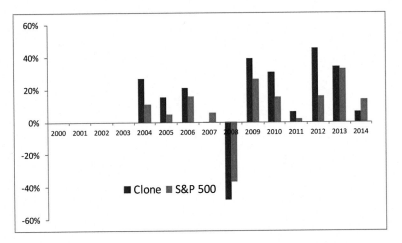

Source: AlphaClone.

LYRICAL ASSET MANAGEMENT, ANDREW WELLINGTON

Andrew Wellington believes bargain stocks are hiding in plain sight. The co-founder of Lyrical Asset Management looks for cheap stocks among the largest and best-known US companies. Unlike many other value investors who believe the best deals are to be found in overlooked, mid-sized or smaller companies, Wellington confines his shopping to the biggest public companies in the country.

"We scan though the top 1,000 stocks that are in the market and look for those stocks that the market is giving away for a great price," he says.

Of course, Wellington doesn't settle for just any stinker. Some companies deserve to have their stock prices beaten down. Wellington looks for companies with sound businesses that have more earning potential than their price implies, and he buys when he finds one whose fair market value is, he believes, about 35 percent more than its trading level. He looks for businesses that are easy to understand and analyze in order to improve his chances of winning. He limits his holdings to about thirty-five stocks and generally holds until his thesis bears fruit, which could take years. "We have no idea when the market is going to recognize value in a company," he says. "We have an indefinite time horizon."

So far, Wellington has proven to be a winner with his system. Lyrical now manages more than $3 billion, and its flagship Lyrical US Value Equity fund was ranked fourteenth on the 2015 *Barron's Penta* Best 100 Hedge Funds. It gained 27.24 percent annualized net since its launch in January 2009 through the end of 2014.

For Wellington, Lyrical represents the culmination of a career spent honing his skills as a stock picker and portfolio manager. A graduate of the University of Pennsylvania, he holds dual bachelor's degrees from the Wharton School and the School of Engineering. He started out in management consulting and had a fortunate meeting with Richard Pzena, a rising star at Sanford Bernstein. When Pzena launched Pzena Investment Management, Wellington joined as a research analyst and rose to portfolio manager. Wellington went on to become portfolio manager at Neuberger Berman and managing director at New Mountain Capital before launching Lyrical in 2009.

Wellington likes to say that he spends a lot of his time looking for companies that are easy to understand and avoiding those that are hard. He does it through deep fundamental analysis, looking to come up with an accurate forecast of future earnings. He figures his chances of getting those forecasts right improve with simpler businesses: "When we see businesses that are difficult to get right, we skip them and keep looking. As I like to explain it, we work really hard to find the easiest investments."

What kinds of companies wind up in the Lyrical portfolio? Recent names have included Goodyear Tire, insurer Aflac, rental car companies Avis and Hertz, and computer maker Dell. One of his biggest wins was AerCap, a company that leases planes to airlines. He started buying it at $3 in 2009. By September 2015, it was trading at $43, and Wellington planned to hold on a while longer. By his calculations, it was still a cheap stock compared to its potential.

We don't have a lot of history for Lyrical, but below are the positions as of the last update.

FIGURE 75 – 13F CURRENT HOLDINGS AS OF SEPTEMBER 30, 2015; PRICE AS OF NOVEMBER 20, 2015

Company	Symbol	Price	% of Portfolio
Avago Technologies Ltd	AVGO	$126.40	5%
Aetna Inc	AET	$104.43	4%
Raytheon Co	RTN	$127.04	4%
Anthem Inc	ANTM	$131.29	4%
Nasdaq Inc	NDAQ	$59.97	4%
Comcast Corp	CMCSA	$62.90	4%
AmTrust Financial Services Inc	AFSI	$61.35	4%
Goodyear Tire & Rubber Co	GT	$34.25	4%
Celanese Corp Series A	CE	$71.30	4%
TE Connectivity Ltd	TEL	$67.61	3%

Source: AlphaClone.

PASSPORT CAPITAL, JOHN BURBANK

Like a lot of hedge fund managers, John Burbank takes fundamental research very seriously. But he breaks with most classic value-oriented managers in the starting point for investment ideas. Instead of a bottom-up approach, Burbank starts at the opposite end, using a top-down, macroeconomic process to point him to potential opportunities at his hedge fund company, Passport Capital.

"The US asset management industry is very good at bottom-up analysis of companies," he said in an interview. "This capability is what distinguishes US investors. I wanted to use that strength, but in combination with what I saw going on in the world more broadly."

That process can lead Burbank to equity investment, but it can also result in his use of more esoteric derivatives that are not available to most investors. His macro approach told him there were problems in the US real estate market back in 2007 and the result was a bet against subprime mortgage-backed securities. Burbank was one of a handful of hedge fund managers who correctly predicted the economic collapse and how to make the most money off it. Passport rose 220 percent in 2007 based on Burbank's contrary bet.

Burbank often makes as much money—or more—on his negative bets as he does on his long stock picks. He tracks and invests in commodities and was initially caught off-guard by the drop in oil prices that began in 2014. But by November, he was betting that oil prices would continue falling into the summer of 2015. It wasn't a straight line, but his view proved accurate.

Passport today manages about $4 billion, and it runs an actively traded portfolio. As of the end of June 2015, Passport owned about two hundred stocks, with some concentration in his top ten. On the company website, Passport offers some insight into its investment philosophy and process. The company says it uses quantitative tools to assist with its macroeconomic analysis and fundamental research. Those quant tools are used to "construct portfolios aimed at delivering superior returns within specific risk and liquidity targets."

Burbank got his undergraduate degree in literature from Duke University and his MBA from Stanford University. After investing on his own for a few years, he joined ValueVest Management, where he rose to director of research. He formed Passport in 2000 in San Francisco and has always maintained a keen interest in Silicon Valley. The Passport Global Fund recorded annualized returns of 17.8 percent from its inception to mid-2015.

Burbank's macro view for the near future envisions a positive environment for solid companies that could continue for years to come. He said in 2015 that he believes he can profit by being long in those companies for the next ten years and that many of them will be technology companies in California.

"My view is that what I call 'A students'—the best students in the class—are who you want to bet on now. You might as well disregard the rest of the class."

FIGURE 76 – 13F CURRENT HOLDINGS AS OF SEPTEMBER 30, 2015; PRICE AS OF NOVEMBER 20, 2015

Company	Symbol	Price	% of Portfolio
CF Industries Holdings Inc	CF	$43.90	11%
SolarCity Corp	SCTY	$29.04	6%
Vipshop Holdings	VIPS	$16.35	6%
Dollar Tree Inc	DLTR	$68.42	6%
Delta Air Lines Inc	DAL	$48.76	6%
Alphabet Inc Class C	GOOG	$756.60	5%
Sempra Energy	SRE	$102.17	5%
Facebook Inc Class A	FB	$107.32	5%
Liberty Global PLC Class C	LBTYK	$40.86	3%
NRG Energy Inc	NRG	$12.00	3%

Source: AlphaClone.

FIGURE 77 – 13F PERFORMANCE, 2/2004–2014

2/2004-2014	Clone	S&P 500
Return	11.60%	7.85%
Volatility	23.03%	14.19%
Sharpe (1.43%)	0.44	0.45
Drawdown	-55.17%	-50.95%

Year	Clone	S&P 500	Difference
2000			
2001			
2002			
2003			
2004			
2005	8.3%	4.9%	3.4%
2006	1.8%	15.8%	-14.0%
2007	18.9%	5.5%	13.4%
2008	-47.5%	-37.0%	-10.5%
2009	58.7%	26.5%	32.2%
2010	25.9%	15.1%	10.8%
2011	-7.5%	2.1%	-9.6%
2012	38.7%	16.0%	22.7%
2013	38.5%	32.4%	6.1%
2014	11.6%	13.7%	-2.1%

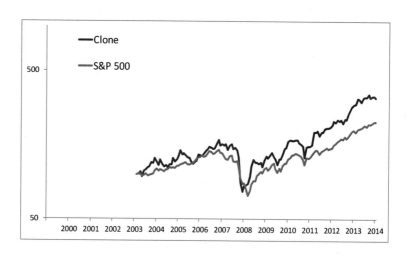

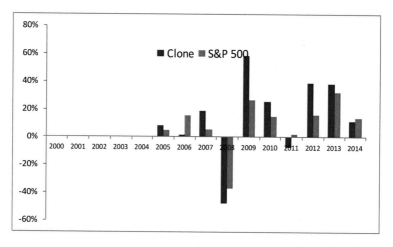

Source: AlphaClone.

PENNANT CAPITAL MANAGEMENT, ALAN FOURNIER

In his book *The Big Short*, which is about the subprime mortgage mess that led to the financial meltdown, author Michael Lewis tells the story of how a handful of money managers figured out the problem and made gargantuan profits by betting against mortgage-backed securities (MBS) with arcane derivatives called credit default swaps. Despite the global nature of the MBS market, the number of hedge fund managers and others who participated in that "big short," Lewis says, was "more than ten, fewer than twenty." One of them was hedge fund manager Alan Fournier.

Fournier, whose Pennant Capital Management runs more than $6 billion, was up more than 40 percent in 2007 on the subprime short. The bet exhibited his willingness to play the markets in ways that may not be popular with many of his peers. His goal: "asymmetric" investments in which he believes the potential return is three times the risk of loss.

While he sometimes dabbles in credit and other strategies, his core competency is as a long-short hedge fund manager, which is how he invests most of his capital. He is a value investor who often looks for deep value, including distressed situations and bankruptcies where he feels he can buy cheap and earn a big payoff in a company's recovery. Unlike some distressed investors who shy away from troubled companies with highly leveraged balance sheets, Fournier will often jump in if he feels the company has a good chance of making a comeback despite its heavy debt load.

Fournier runs several funds with different levels of position concentration. His biggest fund typically carries about 45 long positions, while a more concentrated version runs with about 25. As for favored themes or sectors, Fournier really doesn't have any, preferring to scan the investment landscape in search of the best opportunities he can find, keeping an eye out for anything that might act as a catalyst capable of moving a stock or other instrument, whether that is a macro-economic or market theme or simply a matter of company fundamentals. In stock picking, he uses valuation screens to help highlight opportunities and maintains a healthy dose of short positions in his book. Making money, he says, is a matter of finding undiscovered opportunities by using sound analysis and having enough nerve to stick with bets.

"It's all about setting up those asymmetric bets and getting more of them right than wrong," he once said. "Our losers generally aren't big, and we've had a number of very significant winners. We do well on the short side—earning more on our shorts when the market has been down and losing less when the market has been up. At the end of the day, it's your batting average that counts."

Fournier has done well by that last measure. Since its launch in 2001 through early December 2013, Pennant produced compounded returns of 15.8 percent, versus 3.9 percent for the S&P 500.

Fournier earned his stripes as a long-short equity portfolio manager at David Tepper's Appaloosa Management. He describes his departure from Appaloosa in 2000 as a friendly firing in which Tepper told Fournier it was time for him to leave the nest and run his own fund.

Prior to Appaloosa, Fournier worked for Sanford C. Bernstein, where he got his initial introduction to Wall Street. That job was a career switch for Fournier, who earned a mechanical engineering degree from Wentworth Institute of Technology in Boston and then went to work as a computer salesman for Digital Equipment. Indeed, nothing in his academic or early career suggested his emergence as an important hedge fund manager.

"It's probably somewhat unusual for someone managing a hedge fund, but I've never taken a finance or accounting course," Fournier once said.

Not a bad inspiration for all those amateur investors intimidated by the blue-chip degrees in finance and economics that so many Wall Street mavens hold. What stocks does Fournier like now?

FIGURE 78 – 13F CURRENT HOLDINGS AS OF SEPTEMBER 30, 2015; PRICE AS OF NOVEMBER 20, 2015

Company	Symbol	Price	% of Portfolio
TransDigm Group Inc	TDG	$236.25	6%
Signet Jewelers Ltd	SIG	$137.60	6%
Constellation Brands Inc Class A	STZ	$137.62	5%
NVR Inc	NVR	$1,668.94	5%
WellCare Health Plans Inc	WCG	$79.27	5%
Priceline Group Inc	PCLN	$1,281.53	5%
Marathon Petroleum Corp	MPC	$55.93	4%
Middleby Corp	MIDD	$105.58	4%
Monsanto Co	MON	$96.09	4%
Allergan plc	AGN	$312.46	4%

Source: AlphaClone.

FIGURE 79 – 13F PERFORMANCE, 2/2003–2014

2/2003-2014	Clone	S&P 500
Return	21.74%	9.87%
Volatility	20.24%	13.98%
Sharpe (1.39%)	1.01	0.61
Drawdown	-42.66%	-50.95%

Year	Clone	S&P 500	Difference
2000			
2001			
2002			
2003			
2004	31.0%	10.9%	20.1%
2005	20.5%	4.9%	15.6%
2006	6.1%	15.8%	-9.7%
2007	17.2%	5.5%	11.7%
2008	-26.0%	-37.0%	11.0%
2009	43.6%	26.5%	17.1%
2010	17.3%	15.1%	2.2%
2011	4.9%	2.1%	2.8%
2012	35.9%	16.0%	19.9%
2013	43.3%	32.4%	10.9%
2014	10.8%	13.7%	-2.9%

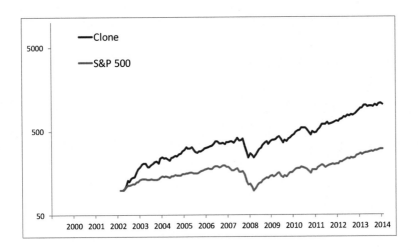

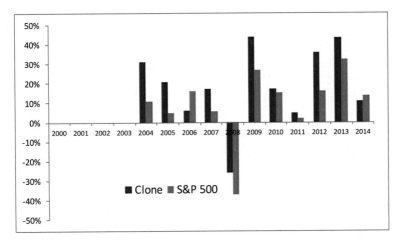

Source: AlphaClone.

PERSHING SQUARE, WILLIAM ACKMAN

"Someone once pointed out that almost everything we've done has been unprecedented."

— BILL ACKMAN

His name is William A. Ackman but everyone calls him Bill, as if he's just a regular guy with a regular job. He's not.

In the noisy world of activist investing, Bill Ackman is one of the loudest. His Pershing Square Capital Management is a hedge fund that manages up to $20 billion and makes huge and outrageous bets that usually—but not always—earn oversize profits for him (Ackman is a billionaire) and his investors. Pershing Square turned a 40% net return in 2014, a year when many other hedge funds struggled.

In photographs and in person, he is a disarming presence, tall and fit with a full head of grey hair and long lashes rimming eyes that seem to twinkle with mischief, an impression that is reinforced by the slight grin he always seems to sport. He has been described as smart and so competitive that he once turned a scuba outing into a contest to see who could use up the least amount of oxygen in their tanks during a dive.

While Ackman has taken some notable short positions, most of his plays are long bets, and he runs a concentrated portfolio of only a few stocks at a time. His investment style is based around deep fundamental research that turns up a key theme or issue in a company that he can then exploit by taking a major position from which he can cajole and bully management into action he thinks will increase value.

"Fundamentally what you're looking for is how much cash the business can generate on a recurring basis over a very long period of time," Ackman once said in an interview. "That's what we do." [29]

You can usually find Ackman in the middle of the biggest and most raucous power struggle on Wall Street. In 2012, he shorted Herbalife, calling the seller of nutritional supplements and personal care products "the best-managed pyramid scheme in the world." The stock initially fell, but then rivals Dan Loeb and Carl Icahn took the long side of the bet, momentarily driving up the price and putting a squeeze on Ackman that left his short play staring at huge potential losses. After rising, Herbalife fell sharply again—good news for Ackman—but then recovered somewhat in 2015. All the while Ackman maintained that the company would ultimately collapse and yield a big payday for Pershing.

One of his most notable recent long plays involved two pharmaceutical companies, Valeant and Allergan. Ackman started out buying Valeant stock, then bought Allergan, then tried to merge Allergan into Valeant. Allergan rebuffed Ackman and opted to merge with another company instead. But Ackman's agitation puffed up Valeant stock so much that Pershing made $2.6 billion in a few months. Those profits have proven illusory, as the stock has declined from $250s to a value of around $100 as of this publication—a decline of approximately 60%.

Ackman holds an MBA from Harvard University and started

out working in his father's real estate company but left to form his first hedge fund, Gotham Partners Management Company, with another Harvard alum, David Berkowitz. After he closed Gotham, Ackman formed Pershing in 2003 and built it into the hedge fund powerhouse it is today.

While he holds a reputation as a somewhat ruthless corporate raider, Ackman thinks of himself as a man of virtue. As he said in a *Vanity Fair* magazine interview, "The single most important thing to me, personally, is the ability to speak my mind. I'm a change-the-world guy, and I know that sounds like bullshit or whatever. I don't like to make investments that are not good for America. You can say I'm self-righteous. You can say that I'm disingenuous. I have more money than I need. I don't need to work for a living. I do this because I love what I do." [30]

As of the time of this writing, Pershing Square is having a challenging 2015 with Ackman's largest holding VRX down over 50% from recent highs.

FIGURE 80 – 13F CURRENT HOLDINGS AS OF SEPTEMBER 30, 2015; PRICE AS OF NOVEMBER 20, 2015

Company	Symbol	Price	% of Portfolio
Valeant Pharmaceuticals Internatio	VRX	$91.00	25%
Air Products and Chemicals Inc	APD	$139.29	19%
Canadian Pacific Railway Ltd	CP	$149.24	14%
Mondelez International Inc Class A	MDLZ	$43.95	13%
Zoetis Inc Class A	ZTS	$47.32	12%
RESTAURANT BRANDS INTL INC	QSR	$ 0.00	10%
Platform Specialty Products Corp	PAH	$11.84	4%
Howard Hughes Corp	HHC	$124.64	3%

Source: AlphaClone.

FIGURE 81 – 13F PERFORMANCE, 2/2006–2014

2/2006-2014	Clone	S&P 500
Return	12.88%	7.75%
Volatility	24.78%	15.32%
Sharpe (1.19%)	0.47	0.43
Drawdown	-55.83%	-50.95%

Year	Clone	S&P 500	Difference
2000			
2001			
2002			
2003			
2004			
2005			
2006			
2007	-12.9%	5.5%	-18.4%
2008	-43.1%	-37.0%	-6.1%
2009	120.2%	26.5%	93.7%
2010	26.2%	15.1%	11.1%
2011	-11.1%	2.1%	-13.2%
2012	26.7%	16.0%	10.7%
2013	20.1%	32.4%	-12.3%
2014	30.8%	13.7%	17.1%

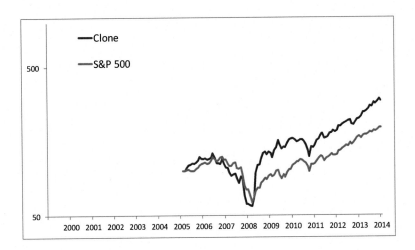

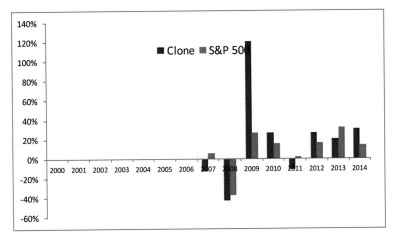

Source: AlphaClone.

RELATIONAL INVESTORS, RALPH WHITWORTH

Ralph Whitworth is not your typical activist investor. From his perch in San Diego, Whitworth has spent nearly two decades buying up shares in companies with problems through his fund company, Relational Investors. He then promotes changes to benefit him and other shareholders, often taking a seat on a corporate board to further his cause.

But instead of being reviled as a greedy profiteer at the expense of troubled companies, Whitworth is lauded as a model corporate steward. In 2014, Forbes suggested that he may be "America's Best Board Member."

His accomplishments include bringing peace to Hewlett-Packard Co. after years of infighting, engineering the replacement of the Home Depot CEO and helping guide the company to improvements and a rising stock price-up, and helping Waste Management navigate its way through an accounting scandal. He has served on the boards of eleven public companies, including Mattel, Sirius Satellite Radio, Genzyme, and Sprint Nextel.

Relational's website describes its philosophy with a quotation from Whitsworth: "We see ourselves as stewards of our clients' shareholdings. Proper stewardship requires active engagement of corporate leadership to spur improved performance."

Founded in 1996, Relational has grown into a $6 billion asset manager that runs a concentrated portfolio designed to get Whitworth heard in the boardrooms of target companies. Although he can sometimes amass as much as 10 percent of a company's shares, he often is able to accomplish his goals by buying up just 1 percent, as he did with HP.

What gives Whitworth so much clout with corporate boards is his background as an expert in corporate governance. From 1986 to 1994, he was president of the United Shareholders Association and successfully lobbied for an overhaul of SEC shareholder rules.

Trained as a lawyer, Whitworth practiced only briefly before becoming an aid to US Senator Paul Laxalt, serving on the staff of the US Senate Judiciary Committee. Whitworth gained his business smarts afterward while working for T. Boone Pickens at Mesa Limited Partners, and he formed Relational in 1996 with another former Mesa executive. Whitworth still says of the oil tycoon, "I learnt more from him than anybody in my business career, and I had more fun working for him than anybody else. I got a PhD in capitalism there."

The types of companies that Relational targets vary widely. As of the first quarter of 2014, Relational held 20 positions, the largest being HP. The rest of his top ten were spread among a variety of companies in various industries, with technology well represented.

Whitworth's plays are by definition long-term, and he can wait years for a payoff. But he has scored enough victories that news of a new position can itself create interest in a company's stock.

Whitworth had something of the sort in mind at Relational. By standing for principles that he championed in his role at the United Shareholders Association, Whitworth hopes to create a sort of Relational "seal of approval" for companies he invests with on corporate governance issues like compensation, capital allocation, and shareholder communications. As he said in a 2008 interview, "You're going to be considered a Relational-friendly company. And you're going to get a higher multiple for that."

Sadly Relational has plans to wind down due to the recurrence of Whitworth's throat cancer. Let's hope he beats it and continues to invest for many more years.

FIGURE 82 – 13F CURRENT HOLDINGS AS OF SEPTEMBER 30, 2015; PRICE AS OF NOVEMBER 20, 2015

Company	Symbol	Price	% of Portfolio
Bunge Ltd	BG	$65.52	43%
Hologic Inc	HOLX	$40.01	35%
Mondelez International Inc Class A	MDLZ	$43.95	12%
SPX FLOW Inc	FLOW	$32.42	4%
PMC-Sierra Inc	PMCS	$11.87	3%
SPDR S&P 500 Trust	SPY	$209.31	2%
SPX Corp	SPXC	$10.90	1%
SPDR S&P MidCap 400	MDY	$263.75	1%

Source: AlphaClone.

FIGURE 83 – 13F PERFORMANCE, 2000–2014

2000-2014	Clone	S&P 500
Return	10.54%	4.31%
Volatility	18.28%	15.24%
Sharpe (1.83%)	0.48	0.16
Drawdown	-53.54%	-50.95%

Year	Clone	S&P 500	Difference
2000	43.7%	-8.2%	51.9%
2001	4.5%	-11.9%	16.4%
2002	-9.6%	-22.1%	12.5%
2003	40.8%	28.7%	12.1%
2004	23.4%	10.9%	12.5%
2005	9.4%	4.9%	4.5%
2006	12.3%	15.8%	-3.5%
2007	-9.3%	5.5%	-14.8%
2008	-41.6%	-37.0%	-4.6%
2009	51.8%	26.5%	25.3%
2010	21.9%	15.1%	6.8%
2011	2.7%	2.1%	0.6%
2012	4.5%	16.0%	-11.5%
2013	43.1%	32.4%	10.7%
2014	3.2%	13.7%	-10.5%

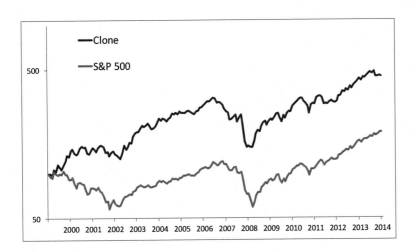

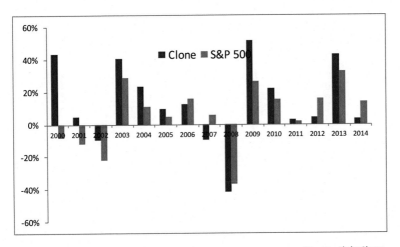

Source: AlphaClone.

VALUEACT CAPITAL, JEFFREY UBBEN

"My father tells me the reason I generate the returns I do is that I see things other people don't see. But that's not exactly the case. I spend my time trying to figure out what the person selling stock to me is afraid of. If I can understand what he's afraid of and it's either irrational or overdone, that's where you can find opportunity."

— JEFFREY UBBEN

For a hedge fund managing about $14 billion in assets in 2014, not much seems to be happening at ValueAct Capital. The firm was holding just fourteen positions at the time, which translates to one monster of a concentrated portfolio.

What's more is that Jeffrey Ubben, founder, CEO and chief investment officer of ValueAct Capital, eschews most hedging techniques that other investors employ, preferring to rely on the wisdom of his picks to protect the downside. And he is willing to wait years to be proven right.

Ubben's theme of value investing with an activist slant (hence the firm's name) has served him and his investors well. He has produced double-digit returns with remarkable consistency since

ValueAct's founding in 2000. Ubben's goal: 20 percent annual returns on his investments' net-of-fees.

ValueAct is designed as a sort of hybrid clone of Warren Buffett, the poster boy for concentrated value investing, and Carl Icahn, one of the great corporate raiders of the day. From his office in a retro brick building in downtown San Francisco, Ubben and his team patiently and methodically examine more than 100 companies each year in search of a few they might deem worthy of investment. His targets are typically out-of-favor companies with sound revenue streams that he believes can hold up in good times or bad and that appear able to grow free cash flow in the future. The object is to get a big enough stake in the company to have a voice in the boardroom, and then to push through some creative reengineering to unlock value that other investors miss.

He states, "We try to focus on businesses that are so good that they're hard to screw up, but many times when management seems to be trying to do just that."

Ubben aims for companies in the $1-$8 billion market cap range and bases his shopping on deep fundamental analysis rather than macroeconomics. As he said in an interview with Value Investor Insight in 2010, "It's frankly an advantage to not get overly distracted by macroeconomic concerns, which can make it hard to pull the trigger on a great business when the opportunity presents itself." [31]

When it settles on a target, ValueAct gradually builds its position over twelve to eighteen months—until it owns as much as 10 to 20 percent of a company's shares. Although ValueAct might suggest replacement of a CEO or the sale of a company, Ubben tries to pitch his ideas with tact. He likes to portray himself as a kinder and gentler version of the more mercurial Icahn.

One contrarian opportunity that presented itself to Ubben in 2013 was Microsoft Corp. Ubben saw promise in a company that many regarded as a tired old relic of a previous tech era. ValueAct started small but increased its position to $2.5 billion.

Within a few months of ValueAct's arrival as a major investor, longtime Microsoft CEO Steve Ballmer resigned and was replaced by Satya Nadella, who Ubben promptly started talking up. Microsoft stock, which had been comatose for years, suddenly perked up, rising about 40 percent.

It wasn't always so seemingly easy for Ubben to move a company and its stock. He laments, "I'm catching a falling sword in almost every situation I'm in, and I'm trying to figure out if it's falling from the second floor or the 10th floor."

When he launched ValueAct in 2000, his actions got little notice, even though he had a solid reputation running a similar portfolio for Blum Capital, another San Francisco investment manager. Before that, he managed the Value Fund for Fidelity Investments, a company he joined after getting his MBA from the Kellogg School of Management at Northwestern University in Chicago.

His most recent forays have tended towards tech and healthcare (note they are another large holder of Valeant stock). But he has also dabbled recently in energy and financials.

Wherever he lands these days, it's likely that Wall Street will be watching.

FIGURE 84 – 13F CURRENT HOLDINGS AS OF SEPTEMBER 30, 2015; PRICE AS OF NOVEMBER 20, 2015

Company	Symbol	Price	% of Portfolio
Microsoft Corp	MSFT	$54.19	19%
Valeant Pharmaceuticals Internatio	VRX	$91.00	16%
Halliburton Co	HAL	$38.00	8%
Twenty-First Century Fox Inc Class I	FOX	$30.54	7%
Baker Hughes Inc	BHI	$51.01	7%
Motorola Solutions Inc	MSI	$72.19	7%
Adobe Systems Inc	ADBE	$91.81	7%
CBRE Group Inc Class A	CBG	$36.86	6%
Agrium Inc	AGU	$95.10	5%
American Express Co	AXP	$72.42	5%

Source: AlphaClone.

FIGURE 85 – 13F PERFORMANCE, 2/2002–2014

2/2002-2014	Clone	S&P 500
Return	21.32%	6.89%
Volatility	18.47%	14.76%
Sharpe (1.41%)	1.08	0.37
Drawdown	-37.32%	-50.95%

Year	Clone	S&P 500	Difference
2000			
2001			
2002			
2003	23.2%	28.7%	-5.5%
2004	48.2%	10.9%	37.3%
2005	28.3%	4.9%	23.4%
2006	17.2%	15.8%	1.4%
2007	-4.1%	5.5%	-9.6%
2008	-19.9%	-37.0%	17.1%
2009	79.9%	26.5%	53.4%
2010	43.5%	15.1%	28.4%
2011	9.7%	2.1%	7.6%
2012	25.3%	16.0%	9.3%
2013	48.2%	32.4%	15.8%
2014	19.6%	13.7%	5.9%

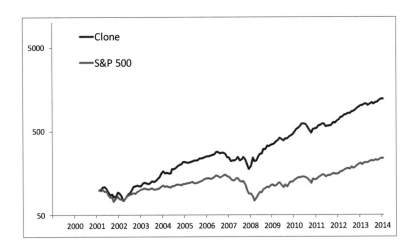

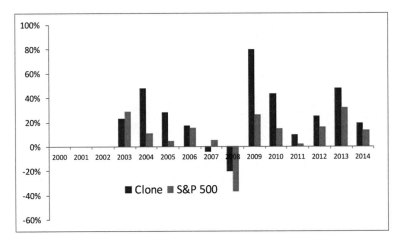

Source: AlphaClone.

NOTES & REFERENCES

1. http://gallery.mailchimp.com/6750faf5c6091bc898da154ff/files/The_
    Capitalism_Distribution_12.12.12_1_.pdf
2. http://www.sec.gov/edgar.shtml
3. http://papers.ssrn.com/sol3/papers.cfm?abstract_id=806246
4. http://www.econ.yale.edu/~af227/pdf/Buffett's%20Alpha%20-%20
    Frazzini,%20Kabiller%20and%20Pedersen.pdf
5. http://www.mebanefaber.com/wp-content/uploads/2009/02/
    wir-winter-2009-february.pdf
6. http://papers.ssrn.com/sol3/papers.cfm?abstract_id=891719
7. http://www.novus.com/blog/analyzing-activist-star-carl-icahn-2/
8. http://avenircorp.com/wordpress/wp-content/uploads/2013/09/
    April_2012_Client_Letter.pdf
9. http://www7.gsb.columbia.edu/video/v/node/1371
10. http://www.designs.valueinvestorinsight.com/bonus/bonuscontent/docs/
    Eagle_Letter2010.pdf
11. http://www.valueinvestorinsight.com/8_06Trial.PDF
12. https://www.greenlightcapital.com/IraSohn2014-final.pdf
13. http://www.novus.com/blog/manager-monday-par-capital-management/
14. http://www.businessinsider.com/dan-loeb-letters-2011-12?op=1
15. http://www.novus.com/blog/manager-monday-third-point-llc/

16. http://www.institutionalinvestorsalpha.com/Article/1914898/Search/
    9-John-Griffin.html?Keywords=john+griffin+blue+ridge&PageMove=6
17. http://www.institutionalinvestorsalpha.com/Article/3472548/Search/
    Lone-Pine-Gets-Its-Groove-Back.html?Keywords=lone+pine
18. http://www.institutionalinvestorsalpha.com/Article/3365982/Search/Lone-
    Pine-Tells-Clients-Loss-Stemmed-from-Sins-of-Omission.html
    ?Keywords=lone+pine&PageMove=2
19. http://www.institutionalinvestorsalpha.com/Article/1961692/
    Julian-Robertson-Jr.html?Print=true
20. http://www.mckinsey.com/insights/corporate_finance/inside_a_hedge_
    fund_an_interview_with_the_managing_partner_of_maverick_capital
21. http://www.forbes.com/profile/andreas-halvorsen/
22. http://www.marketfolly.com/2013/02/viking-globals-andreas-halvorsen-
    rare.html
23. http://www.sec.gov/Archives/edgar/data/1080056/000144738714000065/
    tst1128201413d.txt
24. http://cdn2.insidermonkey.com/blog/wp-content/uploads/2014/06/
    Carlo-Cannell-Letter-to-ValueVision.pdf
25. http://www.institutionalinvestorsalpha.com/Article/3449741/Search/
    The-2015-Rich-List-Christopher-Hohn.html?Keywords=tci+hohn
26. http://www.nytimes.com/2011/04/17/business/17icahn.html?_r=0
27. http://www.investopedia.com/university/greatest/carlicahn.asp
28. http://carlicahn.com/carl-icahn-issues-open-letter-to-tim-cook
29. https://www8.gsb.columbia.edu/valueinvesting/sites/valueinvesting/files/
    Graham%20%20Doddsville_Issue%2023_Final.pdf
30. http://www.vanityfair.com/news/2013/04/bill-ackman-dan-loeb-herbalife
31. http://csinvesting.org/wp-content/uploads/2012/10/
    vii_dec2010_jeffubben.pdf

DISCLAIMER

The views expressed in this book are the personal views of the author only and do not necessarily reflect the views of the author's employer. The views expressed reflect the current views of author as of the date hereof and the author does not undertake to advise you of any changes in the views expressed herein. In addition, the views expressed do not necessarily reflect the opinions of any investment professional at the author's employer, and may not be reflected in the strategies and products that his employer offers. The author's employer may have positions (long or short) or engage in securities transactions that are not consistent with the information and views expressed in this presentation.

The author assumes no duty to, nor undertakes to update forward looking statements. No representation or warranty, express or implied, is made or given by or on behalf of the author, the author's employer or any other person as to the accuracy and completeness or fairness of the information contained in this presentation and no responsibility or liability is accepted for any such information. By accepting this book, the recipient acknowledges its understanding and acceptance of the foregoing statement.